What if the stories your child loved...
also unlocked the skills they'll need
for the future?

CLASS INFINITY

CODE AWAKENED

YEMI AKIN

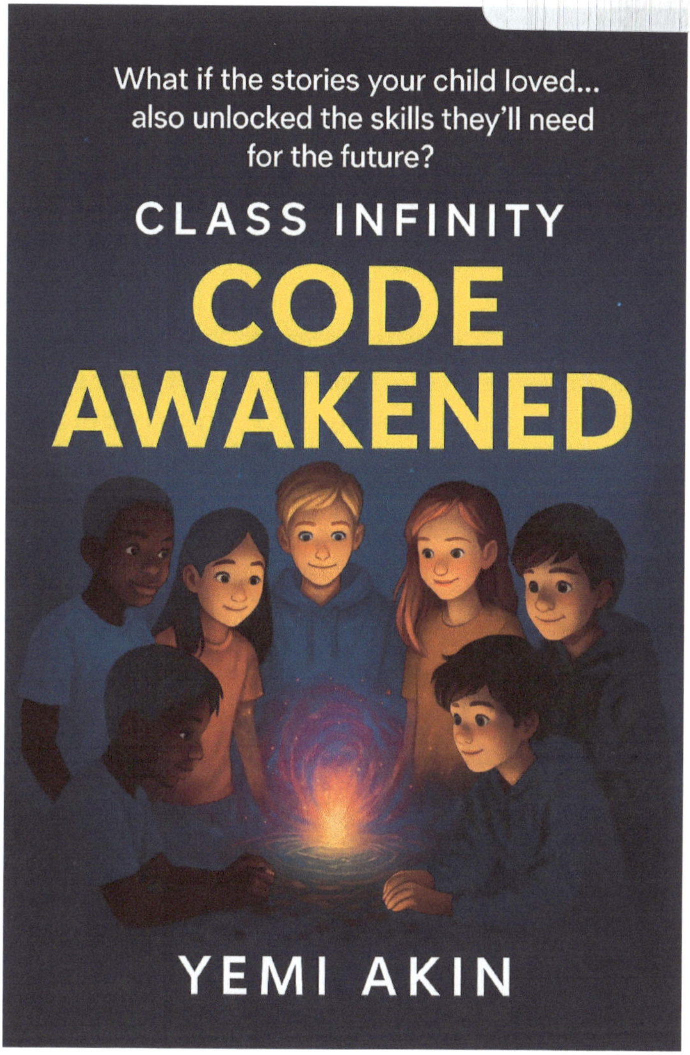

Dear Explorer,

Welcome to your very first step into the world of Artificial Intelligence — the world of ideas that think, tools that learn, and technology that can change lives.

This book is not just about reading. It's about discovering. Creating. Building. It's about awakening something powerful inside you — the ability to imagine and shape the future with the power of your mind.

You don't need to be a genius to begin. You only need curiosity, kindness, and courage. You already have everything it takes to go far — and this book will walk beside you on that journey.

Whether you're reading at home, in school, or with a group of friends, this is your time to explore a world where computers can think, and you can tell them what to do.

So take a deep breath. Relax your shoulders. Smile a little.

The journey is about to begin.

With excitement,

Yemi Akin

"Great explorers don't always have a map — but they do have a mission."

INTRODUCTION: YOUR INVITATION TO THE FUTURE

What if learning felt less like a lesson, and more like stepping through a shimmering portal into a world of infinite possibility? What if the most important skills for tomorrow weren't learned from dusty textbooks, but through thrilling adventures, unexpected friendships, and the quiet magic of understanding how things really work?
Welcome to *Class Infinity: Code Awakened.*

This book is the beginning of an epic journey. It starts not with coding geniuses or straight-A students, but with seven ordinary kids scattered across our globe. There's **Ade** from Nigeria, a natural tinkerer who sees potential in discarded electronics. **Mei-Ling** from China, whose mind sketches complex machines faster than her hand can draw. **Sofia** from Brazil, deeply attuned to the emotions and beauty in the world around her. **Lucas** from Germany, who finds comfort and clarity in logic and structure. **Jayden** from the USA, bursting with impatient energy and a gamer's drive to conquer any challenge. **Samira** from the UK, thoughtful and socially aware, always asking *why*. And **Kenji** from Japan, a quiet observer whose focus on robotics hints at a deep understanding of systems.

They come from different cultures, different backgrounds, and possess different ways of thinking. They weren't chosen for Class Infinity because they had all the answers, but because they carried something far more valuable: **potential**. Curiosity. Creativity. Empathy. Logic. Drive. They represent the diverse sparks of ingenuity found in young minds everywhere.

One day, a mysterious invitation finds each of them, calling them to step beyond their ordinary lives into the **Infinity Nexus** – a breathtaking virtual learning space guided by **M.I.A.**, a kind, wise, and endlessly patient Artificial Intelligence mentor. Here, within this world woven from light and logic, their adventure begins. Guided by M.I.A., they will learn, step-by-step, how to solve problems, build amazing things, and understand the language of the future: code.

What You'll Discover in This First Book:

Class Infinity: Code Awakened is just the first step. As you read alongside Ade, Mei-Ling, and their new friends, you won't just follow their story – you'll learn with them. By the end of this book, you will understand:

- How computers think – following precise, step-by-step instructions created by people.
- The very basics of **Python**, one of the world's most popular and powerful coding languages, starting with the simple magic of the print() command.
- The importance of **sequence**, **comments**, and how to find and fix frustrating (but normal!) **bugs** in your code – the first steps to thinking like a real problem-solver.
- That coding isn't just about typing; it's about logic, creativity, and clear communication.

The Full Vision: A 50-Book Journey to Mastery

This book is portal key number one in a fifty-portal journey. Readers who travel the full path with Class Infinity won't just learn *about* technology; they will grow into **ethical, creative, confident builders** of the future.

Imagine growing up with these characters, sharing their challenges and triumphs. Along the way, you'll naturally

absorb the core concepts of **coding**, **machine learning**, **data science**, **AI agents**, and how complex **AI systems** are designed and trained – all woven seamlessly into stories you love. By the end of the series, you won't just understand the AI age; you'll be equipped with the mindset and skills to thrive within it, becoming an emotionally intelligent, collaborative thinker ready to shape tomorrow.

Who Is This Series For?

- **For kids aged 10–14:** Especially those who feel intimidated by technology, think they're "not good at math," "not smart enough for coding," or simply don't know where to begin. This story is proof that *everyone* has the potential to understand and create.
- **For parents and guardians:** Who know the world is changing rapidly and want to equip their children with relevant, future-proof skills that go beyond rote memorization for exams. This series builds foundational digital literacy and critical thinking in a way that feels like play.
- **For teachers and educators:** Who want to ignite a passion for STEM, AI literacy, and computational thinking in their classrooms but might lack a computer science background themselves. This series provides a narrative gateway, making complex topics accessible and engaging.

Why These Books Matter Right Now:

Let's be honest: the world is transforming at lightning speed. Artificial Intelligence, machine learning, and automation are rapidly becoming as fundamental as reading, writing, and arithmetic were in the past century. Yet, much of our traditional education system was designed for a different era, often preparing students for jobs and challenges that are quickly evolving or disappearing.

Understanding how technology thinks, how algorithms work, and how AI systems are built is no longer optional knowledge for specialists; it's becoming essential literacy for everyone. If our children don't learn to understand, use, and ethically shape these powerful tools, they risk being passively shaped *by* them. This series is designed to empower the next generation to be active participants and architects of their own future.

What Makes *Class Infinity* Different?

This is not a textbook disguised as a story. It's not a dry coding manual filled with jargon.

It *is* an adventure. A tale of friendship across borders, of overcoming self-doubt, of discovering hidden strengths. It's a journey into a world where logic meets imagination, and where learning happens through collaboration, challenge, and moments of breathtaking discovery.

We believe that the best way to learn complex subjects is not through fear or force, but through joy and belonging. Kids who read these books won't just memorize syntax; they will internalize computational thinking. They will feel like heroes on a quest and learn like engineers solving a puzzle. This series aims to break down the fear surrounding AI and coding, building instead a sense of wonder, belief, and excitement. It makes these powerful concepts feel friendly, accessible, and fundamentally *human*.

This isn't just a story — it's a skill set, a confidence booster, and a passport to the world of tomorrow.

Class Infinity starts now. Turn the page, and step through the portal with us.

HOW TO USE THIS BOOK

Welcome, AI Explorer!

This book isn't just about learning how to code — it's your first step toward becoming a world-class AI specialist and agent builder. Together, we'll go from basic Python to building smart AI tools that think, act, and even create!

But first, we need the perfect tool to build with. The good news? You only need one tool for the entire journey — from Book 1 to Book 50. It's called Google Colab.

What Is Google Colab?

It's a free online lab where you can write code, test ideas, train AI models, and even build your own agents — right inside your browser. No installation. No cost. Just your imagination.

Get Started in 3 Simple Steps:

1. **Get a Google Account**

Ask a parent or guardian to help you sign up at:

https://accounts.google.com

2. Open Google Colab

Visit:

https://colab.research.google.com

3. Create Your First Notebook

Click “File” → “New Notebook”.

CHAPTER 1: THE INVISIBLE INVITE

The afternoon sun beat down in Lagos, Nigeria. Heat shimmered above the corrugated iron roofs. Inside a small, cluttered workshop, the air was thick with the smell of warm metal and solder. Ade adjusted his glasses, sweat trickling down his temples. His fingers, usually nimble, fumbled slightly with a tiny screw.

"Almost... almost..." he murmured.

Before him lay his creation: a drone. Not a sleek, store-bought model, but one built from scavenged parts, recycled wires, and sheer determination. Its body was a patchwork of plastic casing and metal strips. Its propellers were carefully balanced fan blades. It was *his*.

He tightened the last screw holding the miniature camera in place. This was the trickiest part. Getting the drone to fly was one thing; getting it to *see* for him was another level. He dreamed of sending it soaring above the bustling markets, capturing views no one else could see from the ground.

He connected the battery pack, his heart thumping a little faster. This was test flight number... well, he'd lost count. Many had ended with a wobble, a crash, or just a stubborn refusal to lift off. But Ade was persistent. Failure wasn't an end; it was just data for the next attempt.

He picked up the controller, another salvaged piece of tech he'd painstakingly rewired. His thumb hovered over the 'on' switch.

"Okay, 'Project Skylark'," he whispered to the drone, "Let's see if you've learned anything."

He flicked the switch.

Nothing happened.

Ade sighed. He checked the battery connection. Solid. He checked the controller wires. Secure. He tapped the drone gently.

"Come on now," he pleaded softly. "Don't be difficult today."

Suddenly, a tiny LED light on the drone's main board, one he hadn't programmed to do anything special yet, began to flicker. Not randomly, but in a steady, rhythmic pulse. Blue. Bright blue.

Ade frowned. "That's... not right."

He leaned closer. The light wasn't just flickering anymore. It seemed to be... projecting something. A faint shimmer appeared in the air just above the drone. Like heat haze, but sharper, more defined.

It coalesced, pixels knitting themselves together out of thin air. Ade blinked, rubbing his eyes. Was the heat getting to him?

No. It was real. A small, glowing rectangle of light hovered above his homemade drone. Text began to appear within it, sharp and clear, written in a font that looked both ancient and futuristic.

You've been selected for Class Infinity.

Are you ready to unlock your mind?

Ade stared, his mouth slightly open. He looked around the workshop. Was someone playing a prank? His older brother, maybe? But Dele was out helping their mother at the market. And this... this technology was beyond anything Ade had ever seen, let alone built.

Selected? Class Infinity? Unlock his mind?

His mind buzzed with questions. Was it real? What did it mean? He, Ade, chosen for something called Class Infinity? He was just a boy tinkering in a hot workshop, dreaming of flight.

Curiosity warred with caution. This felt impossible. Magical. But the drone, *his* drone, was the source of this impossible light.

He reached out a hesitant finger towards the holographic message. It felt warm, humming with a gentle energy.

"Unlock my mind?" he whispered. The words felt strange and exciting on his tongue. He thought of all the things he wanted to learn, the problems he wanted to solve, the skies he wanted to explore. Maybe... maybe this was a chance.

He took a deep breath. "Okay," he said, his voice barely audible but firm. "Yes. I'm ready."

The moment he spoke, the holographic message dissolved into shimmering particles. The blue LED on the drone pulsed brightly once, then dimmed.

And then, the space *before* him began to warp.

Air rippled like water disturbed by a stone. The dusty concrete floor in front of his workbench seemed to dissolve, replaced by a swirling vortex of light and what looked like... code? Green, blue, and silver symbols flowed like a digital river, forming an upright, glowing doorway about his height. It hummed with the same energy as the hologram, pulling gently at the air around it.

Ade gasped. This was real. Impossibly, undeniably real.

He looked back at his workshop, at Project Skylark sitting silently on the bench. This little room held all his dreams so far. But that glowing doorway... it promised something more. Something unknown.

His heart hammered against his ribs. Fear mingled with an exhilarating sense of adventure. He thought of the message: *Unlock your mind.*

He took one last look around, then squared his shoulders. With a determined glint in his eyes, Ade stepped forward, into the swirling light of the digital portal.

Halfway across the world, in a bright, minimalist apartment overlooking the glittering skyline of Shanghai, China, Mei-Ling hunched over her drawing table. Her brow was furrowed in concentration, her hand moving with practiced precision.

Pencil lines, sharp and clean, formed the intricate details of a robotic arm on her large sketchpad. Each joint, each wire, each sensor was rendered with meticulous care. Mei-Ling didn't just draw robots; she designed them in her mind, thinking about how they would move, how they would function. Balance. Efficiency. Elegance. Those were her guiding principles.

Her room was tidy, organized. Tools lay in neat rows. Books on engineering and design were stacked perfectly. Outside, the city hummed with life, but inside, Mei-Ling's focus created a pocket of intense quiet.

She paused, tapping the pencil thoughtfully against her chin. The wrist joint wasn't quite right. It lacked... fluidity. She erased a section, her movements economical.

As she prepared to redraw the lines, something strange happened. The graphite tip of her pencil seemed to... glow. A soft, silvery light pulsed from the point, casting faint shadows on the pristine white paper.

Mei-Ling frowned, holding the pencil up. Had she accidentally bought some kind of novelty pencil? Highly unlikely. She preferred professional-grade tools.

She lowered the pencil back to the sketchpad. The moment it touched the paper, the silvery light flowed out, not as graphite, but as liquid light. It spread across the page, causing the existing sketch lines to shimmer and dissolve.

Mei-Ling watched, utterly still, her usual composure replaced by wide-eyed astonishment. This defied all logic, all principles of physics she knew.

The light gathered in the centre of the page, coalescing. Lines of silver radiance rearranged themselves, forming elegant, glowing characters. It was the same message Ade had seen, rendered in light on her paper canvas.

You've been selected for Class Infinity.

Are you ready to unlock your mind?

Mei-Ling read the words twice. Class Infinity? Selected? Her analytical mind raced, trying to categorize this phenomenon. A projection? Some kind of interactive paper technology she hadn't heard of. It felt... different. More fundamental.

Unlock her mind? She prided herself on her focus, her ability to think clearly and solve complex design problems. What more could be unlocked?

Yet... a flicker of intrigue sparked within her. A challenge. An unknown variable. It was, in its own way, a design problem of the highest order.

She looked from the glowing message to the intricate, half-finished robot design that now seemed mundane by comparison. Her precision, her focus – could they be applied to something... bigger?

A quiet determination settled over her. She didn't speak aloud, but in her mind, the answer was clear. *Yes.*

As if sensing her assent, the glowing words on the sketchpad dissolved. The silvery light detached from the paper, rising into the air before her.

It spun, faster and faster, like a whirlpool of liquid metal. Lines of light stretched and solidified, forming an archway. It wasn't rough like Ade's; this portal shimmered with smooth, flowing lines, like digital ink painting a door into reality. It pulsed with a quiet, contained energy.

Mei-Ling stood up, her back straight. She adjusted her glasses, her usual precise movements returning. This was illogical, impossible, yet undeniably present. Her curiosity, the driving force behind her designs, demanded investigation.

With a calm resolve that masked the rapid beating of her heart, Mei-Ling stepped through the shimmering archway, leaving her quiet room and the Shanghai skyline behind.

Deep within the lush green embrace of the Brazilian rainforest, near Manaus, the air was alive with the symphony of unseen creatures. Chirps, clicks, and rustles filled the humid air. Sofia, vibrant and energetic, crouched low, her tablet held steady.

"Okay, Mr. Monkey," she whispered, zooming in on a tiny marmoset perched on a branch high above. "Show me that funny face again! Just one more time for my channel!"

Her tablet screen showed the marmoset in stunning clarity. Sofia loved capturing the magic of the rainforest, sharing its wonders with the world through her videos. She wasn't just filming; she was telling stories, full of passion and exclamation points. Her bright pink headphones hung around her neck, silent for now as she focused on her subject.

Suddenly, the image on her tablet flickered. Streaks of neon color – pink, green, electric blue – zipped across the screen, momentarily obscuring the marmoset.

"Whoa! Glitch!" Sofia exclaimed, tapping the side of the tablet. "Come on, PiranhaByte," she named all her tech, "don't fail me now! This little guy is pure gold!"

The screen didn't return to normal. Instead, the glitching colors intensified, swirling and dancing. They weren't random anymore. They were forming shapes. Letters.

The vibrant pixels pulsed, arranging themselves into words that glowed against the digital chaos.

You've been selected for Class Infinity.

Are you ready to unlock your mind?

Sofia blinked, lowering the tablet. "Class... Infinity?" She read the words aloud, her voice filled with surprised delight. "Is this like, a new game? An ARG? Awesome!"

She looked around, half expecting to see a hidden camera or another clue. Was this part of some new viral marketing campaign? It felt way too cool for that. The colors on the screen seemed to leap out, full of energy, just like her.

"Unlock my mind?" She grinned. "My mind is already unlocked! It's full of monkeys and jaguars and awesome ideas!"

But still... *selected.* It sounded important. Exclusive. And that name... Class Infinity. It sparked her imagination. What secrets did it hold? What adventures?

"Okay, mysterious screen message!" she declared dramatically to the jungle around her. "Challenge accepted! Let's see what you've got! YES!"

The instant she shouted her acceptance, the tablet screen flared with blinding light, then went dark.

Before her, the air itself seemed to shimmer and twist. The lush green foliage appeared to ripple. Light, the same vibrant pinks, greens, and blues from her screen glitch, wove together like glowing jungle vines. They formed a doorway humming with untamed energy, pulsing like a frantic heartbeat. It illuminated the leaves around it, making the familiar rainforest look suddenly alien and magical.

Sofia gasped, her eyes wide with excitement. "Whoa! Okay, *that* is not a normal glitch!"

Fear wasn't really in Sofia's vocabulary, especially not when adventure called. This was way better than just filming monkeys. This was *happening*.

With a whoop of excitement and her tablet clutched protectively, Sofia didn't hesitate. She plunged into the wildly colorful portal, the sounds of the rainforest fading behind her.

Miles away, in a quiet attic room in Hamburg, Germany, the only light came from the glow of an old laptop screen and a desk lamp illuminating scattered papers filled with complex diagrams. Lucas frowned, tapping impatiently on the keyboard.

Lines of code filled the screen – C++, his current battlefield. He was trying to fix a bug in a physics simulation he'd been working on for weeks. A virtual ball was supposed to bounce realistically, but instead, it kept phasing through the floor. Frustrating.

"Logic error," he muttered, scrolling through the functions. "It *has* to be here somewhere. Collision detection is fine, gravity is constant... where is the flaw?"

He ran the program again. The ball dropped, hit the virtual floor, and vanished. Lucas groaned, running a hand through his messy hair. Skepticism was his default setting. He trusted logic, data, and repeatable results. Things that made sense. This bug did *not* make sense.

As he stared at the offending lines of code, they began to... shift. Characters blurred, rearranging themselves on the screen.

"What now?" he sighed, suspecting a graphics card issue. He tapped the screen.

But the characters weren't glitching randomly. They were deliberately reforming, moving like disciplined soldiers, aligning into perfect rows of stark white text against the black background of his coding environment.

You've been selected for Class Infinity.

Are you ready to unlock your mind?

Lucas froze. He read the message. Then he read it again. His logical brain immediately started searching for explanations.

Malware? A sophisticated hack? Some kind of remote desktop takeover? He checked his network connection – secure. He ran a quick diagnostic – system stable. Nothing explained how text could rewrite itself *within* his active coding window, defying the very rules of the program he was writing.

"Class Infinity," he read aloud, his tone laced with disbelief. "Sounds like nonsense. Marketing spam?" But spam didn't infiltrate code editors like this.

Unlock his mind? He prided himself on his analytical abilities. He solved problems using reason. What did 'unlocking' even mean in this context? It sounded vague, unscientific.

And yet... the impossibility of *how* the message appeared was undeniable. It was a data point that didn't fit any known parameters. His ingrained skepticism demanded he dismiss it, but his equally strong curiosity urged him to investigate the anomaly.

He leaned back in his chair, considering. If this *was* real, what could it be? Advanced AI? A hidden test? The puzzle of it, the sheer illogical nature of the event, was strangely compelling.

"Fine," he said to the glowing screen, a reluctant C++ statement of acceptance. "Conditionally accepted. Let's see the parameters of this... 'Class Infinity'." Define the variables. Show me the data."

The text on the screen dissolved back into his buggy code, but the bug itself seemed... fixed. The cursor blinked expectantly.

Then, beside his desk, the air shimmered. Lines of clean, white light, sharp and precise like perfect code, etched themselves into reality. They formed a rectangular doorway, humming with a low, resonant frequency. It looked stable, structured, almost mathematical.

Lucas pushed his chair back, standing up slowly. His mind still screamed that this was impossible, a hallucination, a dream. But his senses registered the faint vibration in the air, the clear geometric shape of the portal.

It was illogical. It was fascinating.

With a deep breath, steeling his resolve to observe, analyze, and understand, Lucas stepped through the portal made of pure logic and light.

Across the Atlantic, in a suburban garage in California, USA, the sounds of upbeat electronic music filled the air. Jayden, humming along, tightened a strap on the side of a sleek, black headset. Wires, circuit boards, and tiny lenses lay scattered across his workbench in a state of organized chaos.

He was assembling his own custom Virtual Reality headset. Why buy one when you could build something *better*, tailored exactly to your specs? Jayden loved tinkering, taking things apart, putting them back together, making them cooler. He moved with quick, restless energy, always eager for the next step, the next discovery.

"Okay, baby," he said, holding up the headset. "Almost ready to blow my own mind."

He reached for the final component – a small motion sensor. As he picked it up, the twin lenses on the front of the headset suddenly flickered to life. They weren't connected to power yet.

"Huh?" Jayden paused, holding the sensor mid-air.

The lenses glowed with an intense, swirling pattern of electric blue and purple light. Not just *on* the surface, but seemingly *projecting* from within. The light beams shot out, hitting the garage wall opposite his workbench.

The swirling patterns coalesced on the wall, forming bright, pulsating letters, like something straight out of a sci-fi movie.

You've been selected for Class Infinity.

Are you ready to unlock your mind?

"Whoa!" Jayden dropped the sensor back onto the bench, his eyes wide with excitement. "Epic! Is this an Easter egg I accidentally triggered? What did I do?"

He grinned, bouncing on the balls of his feet. Class Infinity! It sounded like the ultimate game, the coolest club ever. Selected?

Heck yeah, he was selected!

"Unlock my mind?" He laughed. "Let's do this! Beam me up, Scotty! Or... whatever you are!"

He pumped his fist in the air. "YES! Absolutely ready!"

The projection on the wall intensified for a second, then vanished. The lenses on the headset went dark.

But the space where the projection had been? It started to glitch. Like a video game tearing, the wall seemed to ripple and distort. Bright, pixelated colors – cyan, magenta, yellow – burst into view, swirling rapidly. They formed a doorway that looked like a shimmering, unstable gateway from a futuristic game, buzzing with playful energy.

Jayden's grin widened. "No way! This is insane!"

He grabbed the partially assembled VR headset, not wanting to leave his precious project behind. Adventure was calling, and Jayden was always the first to answer.

With a running leap and a whoop of pure joy, Jayden jumped straight into the glitching, buzzing portal.

Meanwhile, in a cozy corner of a flat in London, UK, rain pattered against the windowpane. Samira sat curled up in an armchair, a mug of warm chai beside her, lost in a book on her e-reader. The book was about historical figures who fought for justice and equality.

Samira was quiet, observant. She loved stories, especially true ones about people making a difference. Her family spanned two cultures – the vibrant traditions of India and the bustling energy of London – and she often thought about fairness, connection, and how the world could be better. She noticed things others missed, the small details, the unspoken feelings.

She was engrossed in a chapter about challenging unfair laws when the text on her e-reader screen wavered. The crisp black letters seemed to dissolve, replaced by a soft, golden glow.

Samira frowned, tapping the screen. Was the battery dying? No, it was fully charged. She tried turning the page, but the device didn't respond.

The golden glow intensified, forming new words. Not words from her book, but elegant, luminous script that seemed to float just above the screen's surface.

You've been selected for Class Infinity.

Are you ready to unlock your mind?

Samira read the message slowly. Class Infinity. The name sounded vast, mysterious. Selected? Why her? She wasn't a tech whiz or a loud adventurer. She was a reader, a thinker.

Unlock her mind? She thought about the people in her book, how they unlocked new ways of thinking about justice, changing the world with their ideas. Was this something similar? A chance to learn, to understand things on a deeper level?

A quiet curiosity sparked within her thoughtful nature. It wasn't logical, it wasn't in any book she'd ever read, but it felt... significant. There was a pull, a sense of possibility she couldn't ignore.

She looked out at the rainy London street, then back at the glowing screen. Her family often spoke of finding your own path, listening to your inner voice.

Taking a steadying breath, she whispered, "Yes. I think I am ready."

The moment she affirmed it, the e-reader screen went dark. The golden light lifted from it, hovering in the air before her.

It expanded, shimmering like thousands of golden threads weaving themselves together. They formed an archway that looked like turning pages of light, radiating a calm, inviting warmth. It hummed softly, a gentle counterpoint to the rain outside.

Samira stood up, placing her e-reader carefully on the armchair.

She felt a flutter of nervousness, but also a sense of purpose. This was unknown, but it felt... right. Like the start of a new chapter.

With a steady gaze and a thoughtful expression, Samira stepped through the portal of shimmering, golden pages.

In a quiet, meticulously tidy room in Kyoto, Japan, Kenji sat perfectly still on a tatami mat floor. His attention was completely absorbed by the small, six-legged robot beetle scuttling across the polished wooden surface.

He hadn't built this robot, but he had programmed it. Hours were spent refining its walking gait, making its movements seem more natural, more insect-like. Kenji loved details, precision, the quiet beauty of complex systems working in harmony. He found wonder in the small things.

The robotic beetle paused its programmed walk. It stopped directly in front of Kenji, its tiny head tilted slightly. This was not part of its routine.

Kenji watched, his expression calm but curious.

Then, the two small LED lights that served as the beetle's eyes began to glow. Not their usual soft green, but a brilliant, piercing white light. The light intensified, projecting two distinct beams onto the wooden floor before him.

Where the beams hit the floor, the light spread, swirling like liquid crystal. The patterns formed sharp, clear characters.

You've been selected for Class Infinity.

Are you ready to unlock your mind?

Kenji stared at the message projected by his little robot. His quiet focus rarely broke, but his eyes widened slightly. He hadn't programmed this. This was... new data. Unexpected output.

Class Infinity. The words resonated with a sense of boundless potential, much like the intricate code hidden within the simple form of his beetle. Unlock his mind? He always sought to understand things more deeply, to see the patterns beneath the surface. Perhaps this was a new way.

He felt no fear, only a profound sense of wonder. It was like discovering a hidden layer in a program, a secret function he hadn't known existed.

He didn't need to speak. His acceptance was a quiet alignment of his curiosity with this extraordinary event. He gave a small, almost imperceptible nod.

The robotic beetle's eye-lights flashed once, brightly. The projection on the floor dissolved.

In its place, the air itself seemed to construct a doorway. Intricate lines of light, like glowing circuitry or the delicate veins of a leaf, etched themselves into existence. They formed a complex, beautiful archway, humming with a precise, contained energy. It felt both highly technological and strangely organic.

Kenji stood up gracefully. He gave one last look at the robotic beetle, now sitting silently on the floor, its task complete. He felt a connection to whatever force had sent this message through his small creation.

With quiet anticipation, Kenji stepped through the intricate, glowing portal, leaving his serene room behind.

The Infinity Nexus

One by one, seven children stepped out of swirling, shimmering, glitching, glowing doorways made of light and code.

They found themselves not in Lagos, Shanghai, the Amazon, Hamburg, California, London, or Kyoto.

They were somewhere... else.

The ground beneath their feet wasn't solid. It felt like walking on pure light, supportive yet yielding. The air hummed with energy, clean and cool. Above, below, and all around them stretched an endless expanse, not dark, but filled with a soft, ambient glow.

Streams of light, like data flowing through invisible wires, crisscrossed the space in intricate patterns. Glowing geometric shapes – cubes, spheres, pyramids – drifted lazily like clouds. Faint lines of code pulsed rhythmically in the distance, forming vast, shifting walls of information. It was beautiful, awe-inspiring, and utterly alien.

Ade stumbled slightly as he emerged from his pixelated portal, eyes wide, taking in the impossible environment. "Whoa..."

(Page 24)

Mei-Ling stepped out of her archway of digital ink, adjusting her glasses, her analytical mind already trying to map the space, categorize the phenomena.

Sofia burst through her vibrant, vine-like portal, tablet clutched tight. "AWESOME! Look at this place! It's like stepping inside the internet!"

Lucas emerged cautiously from his doorway of pure code, his brow furrowed as he tried to reconcile the sensory input with the laws of physics. "Logically impossible... yet demonstrably real."

Jayden landed with a skid from his glitching game-gateway, VR headset in hand. "Dude! This is graphics level infinity! Where are we?"

Samira stepped gracefully from her portal of turning pages, her expression one of quiet wonder, taking in the streams of light with thoughtful eyes.

Kenji materialized from his intricate circuitry archway, his calm gaze sweeping across the luminous landscape, observing the flow of energy.

For a moment, they just stood there, seven children from seven different corners of the Earth, blinking in the luminous environment.

Then, they saw each other.

Ade saw the girl with the precise look and glasses (Mei-Ling), the energetic girl with the tablet (Sofia), the skeptical-looking boy (Lucas), the excited boy with the headset (Jayden), the thoughtful girl with the warm scarf (Samira), and the quiet, observant boy (Kenji).

Mei-Ling registered the boy with the hopeful eyes (Ade), the bold girl (Sofia), the analytical boy (Lucas), the hyperactive one (Jayden), the calm girl (Samira), and the focused boy (Kenji).

Sofia grinned, waving her tablet. "Hey! Looks like I'm not the only one who got the crazy light-show invite!"

Jayden pumped his fist. "Class Infinity! Is this it? Are we the class?"

Lucas pushed his glasses up his nose. "Seven subjects. Disparate geographical origins. Coordinated arrival. This suggests intelligent design... but by whom?"

Samira offered a small, tentative smile to the others, her mind buzzing with questions but also a sense of connection.

Kenji simply nodded, acknowledging the presence of the others, his gaze curious.

They were different – different backgrounds, different personalities, different ways of seeing the world. Yet, they all shared the same look of astonishment, curiosity, and the undeniable fact that they had all answered the same mysterious call. They had all stepped through a portal triggered by the same message:

You've been selected for Class Infinity.
Are you ready to unlock your mind?

Here they stood, together, at the threshold of something unknown, in a place called the Infinity Nexus. Light pulsed around them. Data flowed. Possibilities felt endless.

What was Class Infinity? Who had chosen them? And what did unlocking their minds truly mean?

The adventure was just beginning.

CHAPTER 2: WELCOME TO THE INFINITY NEXUS

The world dissolved into a rainbow waterfall, colors swirling faster and faster until Ade squeezed his eyes shut. One moment, he was standing in his small workshop in Lagos, the smell of solder and warm plastic in the air, his hand outstretched towards the shimmering screen. The next, the ground beneath his feet felt... different. Solid, yet smooth as polished glass, and strangely cool.

He blinked, his eyes struggling to adjust. Gone was the familiar clutter of circuit boards and wires. Gone was the dusty window overlooking the bustling street.

He was standing on a vast, circular platform made of something like milky glass, lit from within by a soft, white glow. Below the glass, intricate patterns of light pulsed and flowed like lazy rivers of energy. Above him, the space stretched into an impossible darkness, dotted with faint, distant stars that didn't look like any stars he'd ever seen.

Around him, six other kids were appearing, blinking and gasping just like he was.

Jayden, the energetic boy from the USA, landed with a slight stumble but recovered instantly. "Whoa! Awesome!" he yelled, his voice echoing slightly in the huge space. He spun around, arms wide. "Is this like, the ultimate VR? What game is this? Where's the controller?"

Mei-Ling, from China, appeared more gracefully. Her eyes, wide behind her glasses, immediately started scanning every detail. Her fingers twitched, as if she desperately wanted a pencil and sketchbook. "Incredible," she murmured, her gaze fixed on the patterns flowing beneath their feet. "The light pathways... are they conducting something?"

Sofia, the expressive girl from Brazil, gasped, clutching her chest. "It's... beautiful," she whispered, tears welling slightly in her eyes. "It feels... hopeful." She looked around at the others, her expression a mixture of wonder and uncertainty.

Lucas, the logical boy from Germany, was already examining the platform's edge. He tapped his foot lightly on the surface. "Interesting material. Translucent, load-bearing, emits light... How is it powered?" He pushed his glasses up his nose, his brow furrowed in thought.

Samira, from the UK, looked around with a thoughtful, slightly wary expression. She noticed the others, her gaze lingering on each face for a moment. "Hello?" she called out tentatively. "Did everyone else... come through a screen?"

Kenji, the quiet boy from Japan, stood perfectly still, his dark eyes absorbing everything. He wasn't looking up or down, but straight ahead, as if trying to perceive something the others couldn't. His head tilted slightly, like he was listening to a sound just beyond hearing.

Ade took a deep breath, the air clean and cool, without scent. He felt a strange mix of fear and excitement bubbling inside him. He'd always dreamed of places like this, places where technology felt like magic. He looked down at his hands – they looked perfectly normal. He patted his pockets. His favourite multi-tool wasn't there. This wasn't a dream.

"Okay, seriously, where are we?" Jayden demanded, bouncing on the balls of his feet. "Is this the waiting lobby? Are we teaming up? What's the objective?"

"It doesn't feel like a game," Samira said softly, rubbing her arms. "It feels... real. But different."

"The geometry is fascinating," Lucas observed, pointing upwards. "The perceived 'sky' doesn't conform to standard atmospheric scattering. And those aren't stars... perhaps data nodes?"

Mei-Ling nodded slowly. "Or exit points? Or maybe entrances to other... sections?" She knelt, trying to get a closer look at the light patterns under the floor.

Sofia shivered, though it didn't feel cold. "I feel like we're being watched."

As if summoned by her words, the air in the center of the platform began to shimmer. Not like the chaotic swirl of the portals they'd stepped through, but with a gentle, organised energy. Tiny particles of light, like digital dust motes, coalesced, swirling faster and faster, weaving themselves together.

A soft, melodic chime echoed through the space.

The particles formed a shape – a figure made of pure, golden light. It resolved into a humanoid form, about medium height, glowing warmly. It had no distinct face in the human sense, but a smooth, curved head that tilted with unmistakable curiosity. Its body flowed with soft lines of light, and its hands seemed to gesture with grace.

"Greetings, Voyagers," a voice spoke. It wasn't loud, but it filled the space completely, seeming to come from everywhere at once. The voice was calm, clear, and held a tone of warm intelligence, neither strictly male nor female. "Welcome."

The seven kids stared, frozen. Jayden's jaw dropped. Lucas adjusted his glasses again, muttering, "Holographic projection?

Highly sophisticated AI construct?"

Sofia took a half-step back, bumping lightly into Ade. He steadied her, his own eyes wide.

"Who... who are you?" Samira asked, her voice steadier than Ade expected.

The light figure inclined its head. "I am M.I.A. It stands for Mentor and Integrated Assistant. I am here to guide you." The light forming M.I.A. pulsed gently, like a calm heartbeat.

"Mya?" Jayden pronounced it phonetically.

"You may call me Mia, if that is easier," the AI replied smoothly. Its form shimmered slightly, perhaps in amusement. "Names are identifiers, handles for interaction. The sound is less important than the intent."

"Where *are* we?" Lucas asked, getting straight to the point. "This environment... it doesn't obey standard physics."

"A perceptive observation, Lucas," M.I.A. said, turning its glowing head towards him. "You are inside the Infinity Nexus. It is a place built not entirely of matter, but of information and energy. A space where ideas can take form."

"A virtual world?" Ade whispered, his tech-loving heart skipping a beat.

"In a sense," M.I.A. agreed. "But one deeply connected to your world. Think of it as a foundational layer, a place where the building blocks of technology reside, and where new possibilities can be explored."

Mei-Ling stood up, brushing dust that wasn't there off her knees. "The invitation... it said 'Class Infinity'. Is this... a school?"

M.I.A. seemed to brighten slightly. "An excellent question, Mei-Ling. Yes, you could call this a school. A place of learning, discovery, and creation. You seven have been chosen to be the first students of Class Infinity."

"Chosen? Why us?" Sofia asked, her voice filled with wonder. "We're from all over the world."

"Precisely," M.I.A. replied. "You were chosen for your unique minds, your curiosity, your potential. Ade, your intuitive understanding of how things work. Mei-Ling, your gift for visualizing structure. Sofia, your connection to the 'why' behind creation. Lucas, your logical framework. Jayden, your rapid adaptation and drive. Samira, your thoughtful consideration of impact. Kenji, your deep focus and insight into systems."

As M.I.A. spoke each name, its form seemed to subtly shift, acknowledging each of them. The kids looked at each other, surprised and a little embarrassed.

Kenji, who hadn't spoken yet, tilted his head, his gaze fixed on M.I.A. "You know us?" he asked quietly. His voice was soft but clear.

"I know of your potential," M.I.A. clarified gently. "I have observed the ripples of your curiosity in the digital world – the questions you ask, the things you try to build, the problems you ponder. The invitation sought minds like yours, minds ready to learn how to shape the future."

Jayden puffed out his chest slightly. "Okay, cool. So, we're like, special agents? What's the mission?"

M.I.A. emitted another soft chime, a sound like digital laughter. "Your 'mission,' Jayden, is to learn. To understand the language of technology, not just as users, but as creators. To see how simple ideas, careful steps, and logical thinking build the complex tools that shape your world."

M.I.A. gestured with a flowing hand of light, and the vast space around them subtly changed. The platform remained, but the darkness above brightened, revealing the true scale of the Nexus.

It was immense.

Floating in the distance were other platforms, some larger, some smaller. Glowing pathways, like the ones beneath their feet, snaked through the void, connecting them. Huge, translucent screens flickered with cascades of symbols and data. Strange, geometric shapes drifted slowly, pulsing with internal light.

In one area, Ade could see what looked like floating bookshelves, except the 'books' were shimmering cubes of light. In another, complex, shifting puzzles made of light beams hung in the air. Doors made of pure energy stood invitingly, leading to unknown spaces.

"Whoa," breathed Ade. It was like stepping inside the biggest, most complex computer imaginable, but rendered as a beautiful, explorable landscape.

"This is your learning environment," M.I.A. explained. "The Infinity Nexus holds vast libraries of knowledge, interactive challenges, creation sandboxes, and communication hubs. You will learn here, practice here, and eventually, build here."

Mei-Ling was already sketching in the air with her finger, trying to capture the impossible architecture. "It's like a city made of light and thought."

"Precisely, Mei-Ling," M.I.A. affirmed. "And like any city, it operates on rules. Like any machine, it follows instructions."

Lucas peered at a nearby floating icon – a stylized image of a gear turning. "So, this entire Nexus... it's a program? A simulation?"

"It is built upon logic," M.I.A. replied carefully. "The same fundamental logic that humans use to solve problems, to organize thoughts, to give instructions. Think about how you build something in your world. You need a plan, steps, materials. You follow a sequence."

M.I.A. paused, letting the idea sink in. "The technology you use every day – phones, computers, games, even complex machines – is built on that same foundation: human logic, translated into instructions a machine can understand."

Samira frowned slightly. "You mean... coding?"

"Coding is one word for it," M.I.A. agreed. "It is the art and science of giving precise instructions to machines. Telling them exactly what to do, step by step by step. Machines, you see, are very powerful, but they are also very literal. They do exactly what you tell them, no more, no less."

Jayden scoffed. "Yeah, like in games when an NPC walks into a wall over and over 'cause its pathing is messed up."

"An excellent example, Jayden," M.I.A. said, its light pulsing with approval. "That NPC is following its instructions, even when they lead to an illogical outcome in the broader context. The instructions themselves were perhaps incomplete or flawed."

Ade thought about the small robots he tried to build. Sometimes they'd spin in circles or refuse to move. He'd assumed the wiring was bad or a component had failed. But maybe... maybe his instructions, the simple programs he'd tried to load, hadn't been clear enough?

"Let me demonstrate what I mean by 'instructions'," M.I.A. suggested.

It raised one luminous hand. A small cube, also made of shimmering white light, appeared hovering in the air about ten feet away from the group. It glowed softly.

"Observe this Light Cube," M.I.A. said. "It is a simple object within the Nexus. It currently has one instruction: 'Hover in place'."

The kids watched the cube. It hung perfectly still.

"Now," M.I.A. continued, "I want to give it a new set of instructions. I want it to move from its current position, three steps forward – towards you."

M.I.A.'s voice took on a slightly more formal, yet still gentle, tone.

"Instruction One: Identify target destination – three units forward along current vector."
A faint, glowing line projected from the cube, extending three 'steps' towards the children.

"Instruction Two: Initiate movement protocol."
The Light Cube pulsed once.

"Instruction Three: Traverse vector path smoothly over one second."
The cube glided forward along the glowing line, stopping precisely at its end, closer to the group.

"Instruction Four: Cease movement. Resume 'Hover in place' instruction."
The cube stopped perfectly and hung still again.

The kids stared. It seemed simple, yet… profound.

"It… it just did exactly what you said," Sofia breathed, her eyes wide.

"Yes," M.I.A. confirmed. "Precisely what I said. Step by step. If I had only said 'Move forward,' it would not have known how far, how fast, or when to stop. It needs *clear, specific, sequential* instructions."

Lucas nodded slowly, understanding dawning on his face. "So, the Nexus environment itself responds to structured commands. The 'physics' here are based on executable logic."

"You grasp it quickly, Lucas," M.I.A. said warmly. "Everything here, from the largest structures to the smallest particle of light, operates on instructions. And those instructions were written, ultimately, based on human logic."

"Think about telling a friend how to get to your house," M.I.A. elaborated. "You might say, 'Go down the street, turn left at the big tree, and it's the third house on the right.' Your friend understands context. They know what 'down the street' means, they can recognize a 'big tree,' they can count to 'three.' They fill in the gaps."

M.I.A. gestured towards the Light Cube. "A machine, or a program like this cube, doesn't have that context initially. You need to provide every single detail. You need to define 'street,' 'turn left,' 'big tree,' 'house,' and 'right.' You need to tell it *exactly* how many steps to take, *exactly* which direction to turn."

Mei-Ling tapped her chin. "So, coding is like writing a very, very detailed recipe for a robot that can't guess anything?"

"A wonderful analogy, Mei-Ling!" M.I.A. chimed. "A perfect recipe, where every ingredient, every measurement, every action, every temperature, every second is specified. If you miss a step, or write it unclearly, you might end up with... well, perhaps not the cake you intended."

Jayden grinned. "Like that time, I tried baking cookies and used salt instead of sugar. Total fail."

"Exactly!" M.I.A. agreed. "The oven followed your instructions perfectly. The ingredients combined as instructed. The failure was in the instructions themselves."

Ade looked at the glowing cube, then around the vast Nexus. Suddenly, the immense space felt less intimidating and more like... a puzzle. A giant machine waiting for the right instructions.

Kenji spoke again, his quiet voice drawing their attention. "So, this Nexus... it is a place to learn how to write these... instructions?"

"Yes, Kenji," M.I.A. confirmed. "You will learn the languages that allow humans to communicate precise instructions to machines. You will learn how to break down complex problems into small, logical steps. You will learn how to build, test, and refine your instructions until they create the outcome you desire."

Samira looked thoughtful. "So, it's not just about making games or robots... it's about understanding how things work, and how to make them work better? For everyone?"

M.I.A. turned its glowing form towards her, seeming to emanate warmth. "That is the highest goal, Samira. Technology is a tool. Understanding how to wield it gives you the power to solve problems, to connect people, to create beauty, to build a better future. But first, you must learn its language."

The Light Cube, which had been hovering silently, suddenly pulsed again. It performed a little loop-the-loop in the air before returning to its spot, as if showing off.

Jayden laughed. "Can we try? Can I make it do something?"

"Patience, Jayden," M.I.A. chuckled softly. "Your enthusiasm is appreciated. There will be ample opportunity to give instructions, to experiment, to build. You will work individually and together, learning from successes and, just as importantly, from 'bugs' – moments when your instructions don't quite achieve what you intended."

M.I.A. made the Light Cube gently fade away into nothingness.

"This is just the beginning," M.I.A. continued, its voice regaining a touch of formality, but still kind. "The Infinity Nexus is vast, and the journey of learning is long, but infinitely rewarding."

It gestured again, and faint outlines appeared on the platform near the edges – seven distinct circles of light, one for each of them.

"These are your starting points, your personal anchor zones within the Nexus for now," M.I.A. explained. "From here, you will access your first lessons and challenges."

The kids looked at the circles, then at each other. A sense of shared purpose, mingled with nervous excitement, seemed to pass between them. They were really here. This was really happening.

Ade stepped towards one of the circles, feeling a slight hum under his feet as he entered it. It felt... welcoming.

Sofia drifted towards another, a small smile playing on her lips. The fear had faded, replaced by intense curiosity.

Lucas marched directly to a circle, already examining its perimeter. Mei-Ling chose one near him, her eyes still darting around, absorbing details.

Jayden bounced into his circle, eager to start. Samira walked thoughtfully into hers, glancing back at M.I.A. Kenji moved silently into the last one, his posture alert and ready.

M.I.A. surveyed the seven students, its light seeming to glow with satisfaction and anticipation.

"You stand at the threshold of a new understanding," M.I.A. stated, its voice resonating gently. "You have seen a glimpse of this place, a hint of why you are here, and the fundamental idea that precise instructions create precise actions."

The AI paused, allowing the weight of the moment to settle. The vastness of the Nexus seemed to hold its breath.

"You are ready to take your first step."

M.I.A.'s form pulsed with a soft, encouraging light.

"Your first challenge awaits. A simple task, designed to introduce you to the very core of communication within this digital world."

The kids leaned forward slightly in their circles; their attention fully captured. What would it be? A puzzle? A building task? Controlling another light cube?

M.I.A. let the anticipation build for one more moment. Then, its voice became crystal clear, echoing slightly in the immense space.

"But first..."

A collective intake of breath from the seven students.

"...you must learn to speak to the machine."

CHAPTER 3: SAY HELLO TO PYTHON

The seven circles of light hummed softly under their feet, anchoring Ade, Mei-Ling, Sofia, Lucas, Jayden, Samira, and Kenji in the vastness of the Infinity Nexus. M.I.A.'s final words from their introduction still echoed in the luminous space: "...you must learn to speak to the machine."

Speak to the machine? Ade looked around at the glowing pathways, the distant data libraries, the floating geometric puzzles. It felt less like a machine and more like a living galaxy of information. How did you *speak* to something like this?

Jayden bounced impatiently in his circle. "Okay, M.I.A.! Teach us the secret language! Is it like, alien code? Or wizard spells?"

M.I.A.'s light form pulsed with gentle amusement. "Not spells, Jayden, though sometimes it might feel like magic. And not alien, because it was created by humans, right on Earth. We are going to learn a language called **Python**."

"Python?" Sofia tilted her head. "Like the snake?"

"Named after a famous comedy group, actually," M.I.A. clarified, "but yes, the name often makes people think of snakes. Python is a powerful and popular language used for many things in your world – websites, games, science, art, and much more. It's known for being clear to read, which makes it a wonderful place for us to start our journey."

Lucas adjusted his glasses. "Python... I have read about it. It's an interpreted, high-level, general-purpose programming language. Known for its code readability."

M.I.A. turned its glowing head towards him. "Precisely, Lucas. High-level means it's closer to human language than the raw ones and zeros the computer ultimately understands. Think of me, M.I.A., as helping translate your Python instructions into something the Nexus can directly execute."

"So, Python is how we give those step-by-step instructions you showed us?" Samira asked thoughtfully.

"Exactly, Samira," M.I.A. confirmed. "Remember the Light Cube? We gave it clear steps: identify the target, start moving, move smoothly, stop. Python is a language designed to express such steps clearly."

Kenji, quiet as ever, watched M.I.A., his dark eyes focused. He seemed to be absorbing the concept, connecting it to the systems he loved to observe.

Mei-Ling nodded slowly. "So, instead of just *saying* 'move forward three steps', we write it in Python code?"

"That is the core idea," M.I.A. agreed. "And to write this code, you will each need a tool."

With a graceful wave of M.I.A.'s luminous hand, seven objects shimmered into existence, one floating gently in the air in front of each student, right above their glowing circles.

They looked like panes of crystal-clear glass, about the size of a school notebook, but with no visible frame. They hovered silently, catching the light of the Nexus. As the kids looked closer, they saw faint lines of light embedded within the glass, hinting at a keyboard layout, but one made entirely of light.

"Whoa! A light tablet!" Jayden exclaimed, reaching out tentatively. His fingers passed *through* the image of the keyboard, but as they did, the corresponding light-keys pulsed brighter.

"These are your personal Code Boards," M.I.A. explained. "They are your interface with the Nexus, the place where you will write your instructions."

Ade reached out, mimicking typing in the air over the light-keyboard. As his fingers hovered over the 'keys', they glowed softly, and the corresponding letter appeared floating just above the board in neat, white light. He erased it with a hovering gesture near a 'backspace' light-key. It felt surprisingly intuitive, like thinking the letters onto the screen.

Mei-Ling was already examining the layout, her brow furrowed in concentration. "Standard QWERTY layout, but adapted... No physical feedback, interesting."

Sofia laughed softly as she made letters appear and disappear. "It feels like writing on air!"

Lucas was tapping keys systematically. "Latency seems negligible. Direct neural interface, or predictive motion tracking?"

M.I.A. chimed softly. "Let's call it Nexus magic for now, Lucas. The important part is that it allows you to form instructions easily."

Samira typed her name, 'Samira', watching the letters glow. She smiled faintly. It felt personal, yet futuristic.

Kenji didn't type words. He just hovered his fingers over different keys, watching them light up, as if testing the responsiveness of the system itself.

"Alright, team!" Jayden announced, cracking his knuckles in the air above his Code Board. "Let's code! What's the first awesome command?"

M.I.A. turned its attention back to the whole group. "Our very first instruction, our first word in Python, will be one that allows the computer – or in this case, the Nexus – to speak back to you. It's how we make it display words or messages."

The AI paused, letting the anticipation build. "The command is print."

print

The word itself appeared in glowing letters floating beside M.I.A.

"Think of the print command as telling the computer: 'Say this out loud'," M.I.A. explained. "But just like speaking requires more than one word, the print command needs a little more structure to work correctly."

M.I.A. gestured, and more glowing symbols appeared next to the word print.

print()

"First, we need **parentheses ()** right after the word print," M.I.A. continued. "These parentheses hold *what* you want the computer to say."

"And if we want it to say words – what programmers often call ***'text' or a 'string'*** – we need to put those words inside quotation marks ""," M.I.A. added, completing the example.

print("Hello, world!")

The full command now glowed beside the AI.

"This," M.I.A. declared, "is one of the most traditional first programs anyone writes. **print("Hello, world!")**. It's a simple way to confirm that you can make the computer display your message."

M.I.A. gestured towards its own example. "Watch."

The AI didn't seem to type, but the command **print("Hello, world!")** pulsed brightly. Instantly, the words...

Hello, world!

...appeared in the air nearby, shimmering with golden light, about the size of the kids themselves. The letters hung there for a few seconds, vibrant and clear, before slowly fading away like mist.

"Whoa!" gasped Jayden. "It just... appeared!"

"It followed the instruction," M.I.A. stated simply. "The print command told it to display the text inside the quotes, and it did."

Sofia clapped her hands softly. "It's like magic words!"

"It *is* like magic words, in a way," M.I.A. agreed warmly. "But it's magic with rules. The rules are called **syntax**. *Syntax is like the grammar of the programming language.* You need the word print, the parentheses (), and the quotation marks "" around the text, all in the right order."

"Now," M.I.A. said, turning its gaze across the seven students. "It is your turn. Try typing that exact command onto your Code Boards. print("Hello, world!")."

A ripple of focused energy went through the group. Seven pairs of hands hovered over seven glowing Code Boards.

Ade took a deep breath and carefully typed, mimicking the hovering finger movements.
p... r... i... n... t... (
He paused, checking M.I.A.'s example again. Right, the quotes.
"... H... e... l... l... o... ,... ...w... o... r... l... d... !..."
Then the closing parenthesis.
)

He hesitated for a second, then made a gesture like tapping 'Enter'.

Instantly, beside his Code Board, bright blue letters flared into existence:
Hello, world!

"I did it!" Ade whispered, a wide grin spreading across his face. He hadn't expected it to feel so... real. So immediate.

Jayden, naturally, was faster. *Tap-tap-tap* went his fingers in the air.
print("Hello, Nexus!")
He hit 'Enter'.

Hello, Nexus!

"Yes! First try!" Jayden crowed, pumping a fist. "This is easy!"

Sofia typed hers carefully, but changed the message slightly.
print("Hello, beautiful Nexus!")
When she hit 'Enter', shimmering pink letters appeared:
Hello, beautiful Nexus!
She giggled. "They're pink!"

M.I.A. chimed. "The Nexus sometimes reflects the user's intent or personality in the output display. A little personalization."

Samira typed hers exactly as shown:
print("Hello, world!")
Calm, steady cyan letters appeared:
Hello, world!
She nodded, a small smile touching her lips. Simple, clear, effective.

Kenji typed with meticulous precision. Each finger-hover deliberate.
print("Hello, world!")
Deep indigo letters materialized, perfectly formed:
Hello, world!
He didn't smile or react outwardly, but his eyes stayed fixed on the glowing words, studying them intently as they hung in the air.

Lucas typed the command correctly on his first try as well.
print("Hello, world!")
Sharp, white letters appeared:
Hello, world!
He nodded curtly. "Command executed successfully." Then he turned his attention back to M.I.A. "How does the print function interface with the display rendering engine of the Nexus? Is it calling a specific API? What determines the text's persistence and colour?"

M.I.A. pulsed gently. "Excellent questions, Lucas! We will explore the 'how' behind these commands more deeply later. For now, focus on the 'what' – understanding *what* the command does and *how* to write it correctly. That precision is key."

Six of them had succeeded. But Mei-Ling was frowning at her Code Board. She had typed quickly, her mind already racing ahead, but nothing had appeared except for a faint red shimmer around her code and a soft, questioning 'bloop' sound.

On her board glowed:
print("Hello, world!)

She stared at it. "What? Why didn't it work?" she muttered, frustrated. "I typed print... I put the words..."

M.I.A. glided slightly closer to Mei-Ling's circle. "Look closely at your instruction, Mei-Ling. Compare it to the example."

Mei-Ling scanned her code, then M.I.A.'s glowing example: print("Hello, world!"). Her eyes narrowed. "Oh!" she exclaimed softly. "The end! I missed the closing quotation mark!"

Her command was print("Hello, world!) – missing the " before the final).

"Precisely," M.I.A. said kindly. "Remember, the machine is very literal. Python needs both the opening " and the closing " to understand where the text, the 'string', begins and ends. That missing piece confused it. This is called a **syntax error**."

"A syntax error?" Mei-Ling repeated, concentrating.

"Yes. It means the instruction wasn't written following the language's rules, its grammar," M.I.A. explained. "It's like writing a sentence in English without proper punctuation or spelling – someone might not understand what you mean. Computers are much stricter about these rules."

Mei-Ling used the light-keys to add the missing " at the end of her text.
print("Hello, world!")

She hit 'Enter' again.

This time, vibrant orange letters bloomed beside her board:
Hello, world!

A small sigh of relief escaped her. The frustration melted away, replaced by focused satisfaction. "Okay. Precision matters. Every single symbol."

"Got it!" Jayden called out. "No typos allowed! What if I forget the parentheses?" He quickly typed:
print "Jayden rules!"

Another soft 'bloop' and a red shimmer. No text appeared.

"Ah," M.I.A. said. "Another syntax error. The print command in this version of Python always needs the parentheses () to hold what it needs to print, even if it feels obvious to us."

Jayden quickly added them: print("Jayden rules!"). Green text flared: Jayden rules! "Okay, okay, brackets AND quotes. Got it!"

Ade tried printing his name. He typed:
print(Ade)

'Bloop.' Red shimmer. Error. He frowned. "But I used the parentheses?"

"You did," M.I.A. confirmed. "But look at what's *inside* the parentheses. Is Ade text you want displayed literally, or is it something else?"

Ade thought. "It's my name. Text."

"And what did we say text, or strings, need to have around them?" M.I.A. prompted gently.

"Oh! Quotation marks!" Ade quickly edited his code:
print("Ade")

He hit 'Enter'. Bright blue letters appeared:
Ade
He grinned again. "Okay. Text always needs quotes."

"These small mistakes are perfectly normal," M.I.A. reassured them all. "Programmers call them **bugs**. Finding and fixing bugs is a huge part of coding! Don't be discouraged. Each error teaches you more about the rules, about how to communicate clearly with the machine."

M.I.A. gestured expansively. "Now, experiment! Try printing your names, greetings in your languages, simple messages. See what happens. Remember the rules: print, then (), then " " inside for text."

A new wave of energy filled the group as they turned back to their Code Boards, minds buzzing with possibilities.

Jayden, predictably, went for humour:
print("What do you call a lazy kangaroo? Pouch potato!")
Green text flashed the joke. A few soft chuckle-chimes echoed from the other kids' areas as they noticed. Jayden beamed. "Yes! Digital comedian!"

He typed another:
print("Knock knock...")
Knock knock...
Then quickly:
print("Who's there?")
Who's there?
Then:
print("Lettuce.")
Lettuce.
Then:
print("Lettuce who?")
Lettuce who?
Finally:
print("Lettuce in, it's cold out here!")
Lettuce in, it's cold out here!
He cackled.

Samira thought for a moment, then typed carefully:
print("Be the change you wish to see in the world.")
Be the change you wish to see in the world.
It felt meaningful, seeing the words take form like that.

Ade, remembering M.I.A.'s prompt about languages, typed a

greeting from home:
print("Bawo ni, Nexus!")
Bawo ni, Nexus!
It felt good, bringing a piece of his world into this digital space.

Mei-Ling, focused after her earlier error, typed methodically:
print("System analysis: Print command functional.")
System analysis: Print command functional

She nodded. Test successful.

Lucas was experimenting too, but with a different angle. He typed:
print(123)
No quotes this time. He hit 'Enter'.
White numbers appeared: 123
He tried again:
print(10 + 5)
White numbers appeared: 15
"Interesting," he murmured. "So the print function can also display numerical data and evaluate simple mathematical expressions directly, without requiring string conversion via quotation marks."

M.I.A. acknowledged Lucas's discovery. "Indeed, Lucas. Python can work with different *types* of data – text (strings), numbers, and more. The print command is versatile. We will explore data types soon. Excellent observation!"

Meanwhile, Kenji had been quiet. He hadn't typed jokes or quotes. He simply typed one command:
print("...")
He hit 'Enter'. Deep indigo symbols appeared:
...
He stared at the three dots hanging in the air, his expression unreadable but intense, as if contemplating the silent communication, the potential held within that simple output. Then, slowly, he typed another:
print("Awake")
Indigo text: Awake

He watched it until it faded.

For several minutes, the Nexus around the seven students flickered with bursts of colourful, glowing text. Laughter echoed softly as Jayden told another digital joke. Sofia experimented with different symbols. Lucas tested number outputs. Ade and Samira shared thoughtful messages. Mei-Ling confirmed syntax rules. Kenji observed the effects with quiet intensity.

They were no longer just standing in a strange digital world. They were interacting with it. They were making it *speak*.

M.I.A. let them explore, its form glowing with quiet encouragement. Finally, as the flurry of print commands began to slow, the AI spoke again, its voice warm and proud.

"Wonderful exploration, Voyagers. Each of you has successfully given an instruction to the Nexus using the Python language. You told it what to say, and it spoke."

The kids looked up from their Code Boards, a sense of accomplishment shared among them. They had faced the machine, learned its first word, navigated the tricky rules of syntax, and made their own messages appear out of thin air.

"You used the print() command," M.I.A. summarized. "You learned that text, or strings, must be enclosed in quotation marks "". You learned that parentheses () are essential. You encountered syntax errors – bugs! – and learned to fix them by carefully checking the rules."

Ade nodded, feeling a surge of confidence. It wasn't so scary once you understood the pattern.

Mei-Ling felt the satisfying click of understanding. Rules, precision, results. It made sense.

Jayden was already thinking about what else print could do. Could it make sounds? Flashier graphics?

"This is the very beginning," M.I.A. continued. "The print() command is just one small tool in the vast toolkit of Python. But it's a vital one. It allows you to see the results of your instructions, to get feedback, to communicate."

Sofia looked at her Code Board, then back at M.I.A. "So, we can make it say anything?"

"Within the rules of syntax, yes," M.I.A. confirmed. "You provide the instructions; the machine executes them."

Lucas pushed up his glasses. "What other commands are there? Logical operators? Conditional statements? Loops?"

Samira smiled slightly. "It feels powerful. Like we can actually *create* things here."

Kenji gave a single, almost imperceptible nod.

"Your curiosity is exactly what brought you here," M.I.A. said, its light brightening. "There is so much more to learn, so much more you can instruct the machine to do. You can ask it questions, tell it to make decisions, repeat tasks, build complex structures..."

The possibilities seemed to hang in the luminous air around them, as tangible as the glowing text they had just created. They had taken their first step into the world of coding, and it felt exciting, challenging, and full of potential. They were ready for the next instruction, the next puzzle, the next discovery.

M.I.A. let the feeling settle for a moment, the hum of the Nexus seeming to resonate with their newfound understanding. Then, its voice shifted slightly, hinting at the next stage of their learning.

"You've just made the computer speak," M.I.A. stated, acknowledging their success. The AI paused, letting the words sink in before adding the next challenge.

"But what happens if it doesn't listen?"

The seven students looked at M.I.A., intrigued. What did that mean?

M.I.A.'s form seemed to pulse with a new kind of energy, a hint of deeper complexities to come.

"Let’s find out."

CHAPTER 4: POWER IN THE PATTERN

The glow of their successful print commands still seemed to linger in the air of the Infinity Nexus. Ade looked at the spot where his "Bawo ni, Nexus!" had appeared in bright blue, a thrill still buzzing inside him. They had spoken to the machine, and it had answered!

Beside him, Jayden was already fidgeting in his glowing circle. "Okay, M.I.A., that was cool! What's next? Can we make stuff move? Or build a mini-game? Print command is awesome, but I wanna DO stuff!"

M.I.A.'s light form pulsed warmly. "Patience, Jayden. Every complex creation starts with simple steps, learned well. You've learned how to make the Nexus display words. Now, let's see if you can work together to make those words tell a small story... in the right order."

"A story?" Sofia asked, her eyes lighting up. "Like, with pictures made of text?"

"Precisely, Sofia," M.I.A. confirmed. "We're going to use only the print() command you just learned. But this time, you will work as a team. Your challenge: create a tiny 'Digital Celebration' right here in the Nexus."

"A party? Awesome!" Jayden exclaimed.

Lucas pushed up his glasses. "Objective: Simulate a celebratory event using sequential print function calls. Parameters?"

"Simplicity is key," M.I.A. replied. "Each of you will contribute one or two print commands to add an element to the celebration. Think about what makes a celebration fun."

M.I.A. turned its gentle, glowing gaze to each student.

"Sofia, perhaps you could create some decorations? Banners, balloons, using text and symbols?"
Sofia nodded eagerly, already picturing sparkling text banners.

"Jayden, celebrations often have excitement, maybe some confetti?"
Jayden grinned. "Confetti made of code? I can do that! Pow! Boom!"

"Mei-Ling, every event needs a clear start. Maybe a welcome message or a title?"
Mei-Ling nodded, already thinking about neat, centered text. "Understood. A clear identifier."

"Lucas, what's a celebration without a treat? Could you design a small cake using text characters?"
Lucas considered this. "ASCII art representation of a cake. Logically feasible. I will attempt a two-layer structure."

"Ade, celebrations often have music. Can you represent that with text?"
Ade thought for a moment. "Like, printing musical notes or saying music is playing? Yes, I can try."

"Samira, a celebration should have meaning. Perhaps a final, positive message for everyone?"
Samira smiled softly. "A message about togetherness? I like that."

"And Kenji," M.I.A. turned to the quietest member. "Maybe you can signal the very beginning? Like the lights coming up on a stage?"
Kenji gave a slight nod, his eyes thoughtful. "A start signal."

"Excellent," M.I.A. said. "Now, go ahead. Use your Code Boards. Type your print() command, or commands, to create your part of the celebration. Remember the rules: print(), with text inside quotation marks "". Take your time, make it look how you want."

A buzz of activity filled the space. Fingers hovered and danced over the light-keyboards.

Sofia typed carefully:

```
print("~~~***~~~***~~~***~~~")
print("oOo WELCOME! oOo")
print("~~~***~~~***~~~***~~~")
```

She imagined them as shimmering banners.

Jayden went for enthusiastic chaos:

```
print("*!* WOW! *!*")
print("!*!*!*!*!*!")
print("*!* PARTY! *!*")
```

Virtual confetti!

Mei-Ling aimed for clarity:

```
print("=================================")
print(" Digital Celebration Start! ")
print("=================================")
```

A perfect title card.

Lucas meticulously constructed his cake:

```
print(" .--. ")
print(" |====| ")
print(" .'----'. ")
print(" |______| ")
```

He checked the alignment carefully. ASCII art required precision.

Ade typed his musical cue:

```
print("♪♪♪ Happy Music Begins! ♪♪♪")
```

He hoped the little note symbols would show up.

Samira thought about her message, then typed:

```
print("Learning together is something to celebrate!")
```

A simple, positive thought.

Kenji typed his signal, minimal and direct:

print("--- START ---")
Just enough to mark the beginning.

Within a few minutes, they all finished, looking pleased with their individual contributions. Their code snippets glowed on their respective Code Boards.

"Okay, M.I.A., we're ready!" Jayden announced, bouncing slightly. "Let's see our awesome party!"

"Very well," M.I.A. said. "You have all written your instructions. Now, let's feed them to the Nexus and see the result. Execute commands!"

M.I.A. gestured, and the Nexus seemed to gather the code from their boards. There was a brief pause, a hum of energy, and then... chaos erupted.

Suddenly, flashing directly in the center of the platform, bright green letters screamed:

```
*!* WOW! *!*
!*!*!*!*!*!
*!* PARTY! *!*
```

Jayden's confetti exploded first, raining down exclamation points and asterisks into empty space.

Then, slightly overlapping the bottom of the confetti text, Lucas's white cake appeared:

```
.--.
|====|
.'----'.
|______|
```

A cake, sitting forlornly amidst raining symbols.

Before the cake fully formed, Ade's blue musical cue popped up right next to it:
♪♪♪ Happy Music Begins! ♪♪♪
The music was apparently starting before anyone had arrived or anything was set up.

Then, Kenji's deep indigo signal appeared *below* everything else, almost lost:
--- START ---
The start signal... after the party and cake?

Almost immediately, Samira's thoughtful cyan message materialized, slightly overlapping the 'music':
Learning together is something to celebrate!
A nice closing thought appearing randomly in the middle.

Finally, as if an afterthought, Sofia's pink banners flickered into existence *above* the messy pile of text:
~~~***~~~***~~~***~~~
oOo WELCOME! oOo
~~~***~~~***~~~***~~~

The welcome banner, welcoming everyone to the jumbled confusion beneath it.

And last but not least, Mei-Ling's neat orange title card appeared, jammed right in the middle of everything, overwriting parts of the cake and confetti:
==============================
Digital Celebration Start!
==============================

The result was a bewildering, overlapping mess of text in different colours and styles. Confetti rained down on a cake while music played for no one, next to a closing message, underneath a welcome banner, with the start signal hidden at the bottom and the title card splattered across the middle.

It looked less like a celebration and more like a program had sneezed.

There was a moment of stunned silence.

Then, Jayden burst out laughing. He doubled over, pointing at the jumbled text. "Whoa! What WAS that? The cake exploded before the party even started! And the music! Haha! Epic fail!"

Sofia stared, aghast. "My banners! They're all messy! And the welcome is on top of the cake!" She looked genuinely distressed by the visual chaos.

Ade blinked, confused. "The music came way too early..."

"The structural integrity of the event simulation is compromised," Lucas stated flatly, adjusting his glasses. "Analysis indicates a non-sequential execution of submitted code blocks."

Mei-Ling frowned, tapping her finger against her chin. "It's completely out of order. The title card appeared last! That makes no logical sense for a celebration."

Samira looked at the jumble, then at M.I.A. "It... didn't understand what we *wanted* it to do, did it? It just... did the steps we gave it, somehow."

Kenji simply watched the chaotic display, his expression unreadable, but his head tilted slightly as if analyzing the pattern of the failure.

M.I.A. let them react for a moment, the chaotic text slowly fading. Then, its light pulsed calmly. "An interesting result, wouldn't you agree?"

"Interesting? It was a disaster!" Sofia exclaimed, though Jayden was still chuckling.

"It was not the celebration you intended," M.I.A. acknowledged gently. "But Jayden's reaction is also valid – sometimes unexpected results can be informative, even amusing. The important question is: *Why* did this happen?"

Lucas spoke up. "The system executed the print commands, but not in the intended sequence. It appears to have processed them in an arbitrary or perhaps asynchronous order based on submission time or internal queuing."

"You are very close, Lucas," M.I.A. said. "Let's simplify. The Nexus, like any computer, is a machine that follows instructions. It received seven sets of print commands from you. It did exactly what you told it to do: it printed everything."

M.I.A. paused, letting the core idea sink in. "But... you didn't tell it the **order**. You each created your piece, but you didn't define the sequence, the *pattern*, for how those pieces should fit together."

"So, it just ran them... whenever?" Ade asked.

"It ran them in the order it processed them, which wasn't the order needed for a logical celebration," M.I.A. explained. "Imagine building with blocks. If you put the roof on first, then try to build the walls underneath, the whole thing collapses. The *order* matters."

"It's like trying to eat dessert before the main course, then setting the table afterwards," Samira mused. "It just doesn't work properly."

"An excellent analogy, Samira," M.I.A. praised. "Computers don't 'know' that a welcome message should come before confetti. They don't understand context or intention unless we provide it through clear, **sequential** instructions."

"Sequence," Mei-Ling murmured, realization dawning on her face. "We needed to define the steps. Step 1, Step 2, Step 3..."

"Precisely, Mei-Ling!" M.I.A. chimed. "Programming isn't just about knowing the commands like print. It's about arranging those commands in the correct order to achieve the desired result. That ordered set of instructions is sometimes called an **algorithm**."

"An algorithm is just... the steps?" Ade asked.

"A clear, step-by-step procedure for solving a problem or completing a task," M.I.A. confirmed. "Like a recipe, or assembly instructions, or the rules for a game. The order is crucial."

M.I.A. gestured towards their Code Boards, which had cleared. "Let's try this again. But first, let's plan our sequence. What needs to happen first in our Digital Celebration?"

"The start signal!" Jayden shouted. "Kenji's thing!"

"Okay," M.I.A. agreed. "Step 1: Kenji's print("--- START ---"). What comes next?"

"My title card!" Mei-Ling said immediately. "To announce the event."
"Step 2: Mei-Ling's print commands for the title," M.I.A. noted.

"Then decorations!" Sofia insisted. "You need to set the scene."
"Step 3: Sofia's banners and welcome message," M.I.A. continued.

"Music!" Ade suggested. "Once it looks like a party, you need music."
"Step 4: Ade's print("♪♪♪ Happy Music Begins! ♪♪♪")."

"Cake time!" Jayden yelled.
Lucas nodded. "Step 5: Display the cake ASCII art."

"Then confetti!" Jayden bounced. "To celebrate the cake!"
"Step 6: Jayden's print commands for confetti."

"And finally," Samira added, "the closing message."
"Step 7: Samira's print("Learning together is something to celebrate!")."

M.I.A. seemed to shimmer with approval. "Excellent teamwork! You have now defined the **sequence**, the logical flow for your celebration. You've created a simple algorithm."

The AI made a subtle adjustment to their Code Boards. "I have linked your boards temporarily. Now, re-enter your exact same print commands. But this time, the Nexus understands the order you just decided upon. It will execute Step 1, then Step 2, then Step 3, and so on. Kenji, please enter your command first."

Kenji typed: print("--- START ---") and hit 'Enter'.

Instantly, the indigo text appeared, clean and clear in the center:
--- START ---

"Mei-Ling, Step 2," M.I.A. prompted.
Mei-Ling typed her title card commands. The orange text

appeared neatly below Kenji's signal:
==================================
Digital Celebration Start!
==================================

"Sofia, Step 3."
Sofia typed her banner commands. The pink text framed the title card beautifully:
~~~***~~~***~~~***~~~
oOo WELCOME! oOo
~~~***~~~***~~~***~~~
She sighed happily. "Much better!"

"Ade, Step 4."
Ade typed. The blue music cue appeared below the banners:
♪♪♪ Happy Music Begins! ♪♪♪

"Lucas, Step 5."
Lucas typed his cake code. The white text art materialized perfectly below the music line:
.--.
|====|
.'----'.
|______|
"Cake deployment successful," Lucas reported.

"Jayden, Step 6!"
Jayden eagerly typed his confetti commands. This time, the green symbols rained down *around* the cake and banners, like actual celebration confetti:
! WOW! *!*
!*!*!*!*!*!
! PARTY! *!*
"Yeah! Now that's confetti!" Jayden cheered.

"And Samira, Step 7, conclude our celebration."
Samira typed her message. The cyan text appeared neatly at the very bottom, a perfect final touch:
Learning together is something to celebrate!

The complete Digital Celebration glowed before them – organised, clear, and looking exactly like they had intended. The banners welcomed them, the title announced the event, the music played, the cake sat proudly, the confetti showered down, and the final message resonated warmly.

It worked.

A collective sigh of satisfaction went through the group.

"Whoa," Ade breathed. "It looks completely different, just by changing the order."

"The power of sequence," M.I.A. stated softly. "You used the exact same commands as before. The only difference was the **order** in which they were executed."

"So, coding isn't just about knowing the words," Samira reflected, looking at the successful celebration. "It's about knowing the right steps, in the right order. Like planning a project, or even just explaining something clearly to someone."

"Exactly," M.I.A. affirmed. "Computers, AI, games, websites, the apps on your phones – they all run on instructions created by humans. And those instructions must be in a precise, logical sequence to work correctly. A single step out of place can cause unexpected 'bugs' or complete failure, just like you saw with your first attempt."

Jayden, surprisingly thoughtful now, nodded. "Yeah, like in a game, if the 'Game Over' screen showed up *before* the final boss fight, that would be totally messed up. The order has to be right."

Mei-Ling looked pleased. "Listing the steps first – defining the algorithm – saved us time and prevented errors on the second try."

Sofia beamed at the harmonious digital display. "And when the order is right, it looks beautiful!"

Lucas adjusted his glasses again. "The sequential execution model is fundamental. Understanding flow control is critical for any complex programming."

Kenji observed the perfectly ordered text, then gave another tiny, almost imperceptible nod. Order achieved.

The successful celebration glowed for a few more moments before gently fading, leaving the vast Nexus platform clear once more. The lesson, however, remained bright in their minds. They hadn't just learned print(); they had learned that the *pattern* of instructions was just as important as the instructions themselves. They had seen firsthand how computers think – or rather, how they *don't* think, simply executing commands one after another.

They had felt the frustration of chaos and the satisfaction of order. They had glimpsed the fundamental logic that powered the digital world.

M.I.A. let the understanding settle, its form radiating quiet pride in its new students. They were learning not just commands, but concepts.

"You have taken another vital step," M.I.A. said, its voice warm and encouraging. "You understand that sequence is power. The careful arrangement of simple steps can build wonderful, complex things."

The AI paused, turning its glowing form slightly, hinting at the path ahead.

"Every great program, every helpful app, every complex AI starts with the right steps, laid out in the right order."

M.I.A.'s voice filled the space, sparking curiosity for the next lesson.

"Now... let's learn how to write those steps down even more clearly."

CHAPTER 5: LEAVE A MESSAGE BEHIND

The digital glow of their successful, ordered 'Celebration' from Chapter 4 still warmed the air in the Infinity Nexus. They had done it! By putting their print() commands in the right sequence, they had turned chaos into creation. Ade smiled, remembering the perfectly formed text-cake and the confetti raining down just right. Order felt good.

"Sequence is power," M.I.A.'s calm voice echoed, reminding them of their last lesson. "Arranging instructions correctly allows you to build amazing things. But today, we explore a different kind of power – the power of understanding."

Jayden squinted at the AI. "Understanding? Don't we already understand? We made the party work!"

"You understand the code *you just wrote*," M.I.A. clarified gently. "But what happens when code gets complex? What happens when you look back at code you wrote weeks ago? Or, even more importantly, what happens when someone *else* needs to read and understand *your* code?"

Lucas adjusted his glasses. "Code documentation. Essential for maintainability and collaborative development."

M.I.A. pulsed approvingly. "Precisely, Lucas. Imagine finding an old map," the AI continued, turning to the others. "It shows lines and symbols, maybe rivers and mountains. But without a legend, without notes explaining what the symbols *mean*, the map might be confusing, even useless."

Sofia nodded slowly. "Like if you don't know if a squiggly line is a river or a dangerous path."

"Exactly," M.I.A. said. "Code can be like that map. The commands tell the computer *what* to do, but sometimes humans need help understanding *why*."

Ade thought about the complex circuits he tinkered with back home. Sometimes he'd forget why he'd connected a certain wire a certain way. He'd have to trace everything back, wasting time. Notes would have helped.

"So, how do we leave notes in code?" Samira asked. "Won't that mess up the instructions for the computer?"

"An excellent question, Samira," M.I.A. replied. "You need a way to write messages that the computer completely ignores, but that humans can read. Python, like many languages, has a special symbol for this."

With a gesture from M.I.A., a symbol appeared in glowing light beside it:

```
#
```

"This symbol," M.I.A. explained, "is called a hash sign, or sometimes a pound sign or number sign on your keyboards. In Python, when you put a # on a line, everything *after* that symbol on the same line is considered a **comment**."

 # This is a comment.
The example glowed brightly.

"The computer sees the # and skips the rest of the line entirely," M.I.A. continued. "It doesn't try to run it as an instruction. But humans? We can read it!"

"So it's like... invisible ink for the computer?" Jayden asked, intrigued.

"A good way to think about it!" M.I.A. chimed. "Invisible instructions for the computer, but visible notes for people. You can use comments to explain what a piece of code does, why you wrote it that way, or leave reminders for yourself or your teammates."

M.I.A. showed another example, adapting one of their celebration lines:

```
print("oOo WELCOME! oOo") # Display the main welcome banner
```

"See?" M.I.A. pointed out. "The computer still runs **print("oOo WELCOME! oOo")** perfectly. But the comment # Display the main welcome banner helps a human reader understand the purpose of that line."

"It's like writing notes in the margin of a book!" Sofia exclaimed.

"Or labelling the wires in a circuit!" Ade added.

"Or keeping a logbook during an experiment," Lucas stated.

Mei-Ling nodded thoughtfully. "A way to embed explanations directly within the code structure. Efficient."

Kenji tilted his head, perhaps contemplating the idea of hidden messages within functional systems.

"Comments make code easier to understand, easier to fix if something goes wrong (we call that 'debugging'), and much easier to work on as a team," M.I.A. summarized.

"Let me show you why this matters," M.I.A. said. The AI waved a hand, and a block of code appeared, floating in the center of the Nexus. It was the code for their successful 'Digital Celebration', but stripped bare.

```
    print("--- START ---")
print("==============================")
print("  Digital Celebration Start!  ")
print("==============================")
```

```
print("~~~***~~~***~~~***~~~")
print("oOo WELCOME! oOo")
print("~~~***~~~***~~~***~~~")
print("♪♪♪ Happy Music Begins! ♪♪♪")
print("  .--.  ")
print(" |====| ")
print(" .'----'. ")
print(" |______| ")
print("*!* WOW! *!*")
print("!*!*!*!*!*!")
print("*!* PARTY! *!*")
print("Learning together is something to celebrate!")
```

"This code works perfectly," M.I.A. stated. "It produces the celebration you designed. But imagine you are seeing it for the first time. Or imagine it was much, much longer – hundreds or thousands of lines. Could you immediately tell what each part does? Why the .--. is there? What the *!* lines represent?"

The kids looked at the plain code. It felt... colder, somehow, less meaningful without the memory of who wrote each part and why.

"I mean, we remember *now* because we just did it," Jayden admitted. "But if this was next week? Or if it was way bigger? Probably not."

"Exactly," M.I.A. said. "Now, observe."

The code shimmered, and comments appeared next to each section, written in a soft grey light:

```
    # Signal the beginning of the event
print("--- START ---")
```

```
# Display the main title card
print("==============================")
print("  Digital Celebration Start!  ")
print("==============================")

# Show decorative banners and welcome text
print("~~~***~~~***~~~***~~~")
print("oOo WELCOME! oOo")
print("~~~***~~~***~~~***~~~")

# Indicate that music is starting
print("♪♪♪ Happy Music Begins! ♪♪♪")

# Draw a two-layer cake using text characters (ASCII art)
print("  .--.  ")
print(" |====| ")
print(" .'----'. ")
print(" |______| ")

# Create a burst of confetti excitement
print("*!* WOW! *!*")
print("!*!*!*!*!*!")
print("*!* PARTY! *!*")

# Display the final concluding message
print("Learning together is something to celebrate!")
```

"Ah," Sofia breathed. "Now it makes sense again! The comments are like little labels."

"They explain the *purpose*," Mei-Ling added. "Not just the action."

"Clarity restored," Lucas confirmed.

"Comments are essential for communication," M.I.A. emphasized. "Coding isn't just about talking to the computer; it's also about talking to other humans, including your future self. Now, let's practice this communication with a new challenge: **Team Code Relays**."

A ripple of excitement went through the group.

"Here's how it works," M.I.A. explained. "I will divide you into two teams. Each team will work together to build a simple scene using only print() commands, just like our celebration. But here's the twist: you will build it one line at a time, like a relay race."

M.I.A. continued, "The first person on the team adds one print() line to start the scene. Crucially, they must also add one **# comment explaining** ***what their line does or why they added it.*** Then, they 'pass' the code to the next teammate. That person sees the code and the comment, adds their own single line of print() code and their own explanatory comment, and passes it on."

"So we only see the code and the last comment?" Ade clarified.

"You will see all the previous code and comments," M.I.A. confirmed. "The comments are your main way of understanding what your teammates intended, helping you decide what to add next. The goal is to create a coherent scene together, using comments to guide each other."

Two areas on the main platform glowed softly, labelled 'Team Alpha' and 'Team Beta'.

"Team Alpha," M.I.A. announced, "will be Ade, Mei-Ling, Jayden, and Kenji." Ade gave Mei-Ling a nod. Jayden grinned at Kenji, who offered a slight, almost imperceptible dip of his head in return.

"Team Beta," M.I.A. continued, "will be Sofia, Lucas, and Samira." Sofia waved enthusiastically at Lucas and Samira. Lucas gave a curt nod, while Samira offered a warm smile.

"Team Alpha will build a simple picture of a tree in a park. Team Beta will build a simple picture of a friendly robot. Begin with the first person on each team. Add your line and your comment, then signal you are ready to pass."

Team Alpha - Turn 1: Ade

Ade, being first, thought for a moment. A park scene needs ground. He typed onto his Code Board:

```
print("--------------------") # Draw the ground line for our park scene
```

He checked his code and comment. Clear and simple. "Okay, Team Alpha, line 1 done. Passing to Mei-Ling!" he announced. The code shimmered and appeared on Mei-Ling's board.Team Alpha - Turn 2: Mei-Ling

Mei-Ling saw Ade's line and comment. Logical start. A park needs trees. She decided to start the trunk.

```
print("--------------------") # Draw the ground line for our park scene
print("     ||     ") # Start the trunk of the tree in the middle
```

She made sure the trunk was centered above the ground line. "Trunk started," she stated crisply. "Passing to Jayden." The code transferred.

Team Alpha - Turn 3: Jayden

Jayden saw the ground and the small trunk. "Okay, tree needs... action!" he thought. He quickly typed:

```
print("--------------------") # Draw the ground line for our park scene
print("     ||     ") # Start the trunk of the tree in the middle
```

```
print("     *zap!*     ")
```

He grinned, imagining a lightning strike near the tree for drama. But he was so focused on the 'zap!' that he forgot the comment! "Done! Passing to Kenji!" he yelled. The code, now with the uncommented 'zap!', appeared on Kenji's board.

Team Alpha - Turn 4: Kenji

Kenji stared intently at the code. He saw the ground **(# Draw the ground...).** He saw the trunk **(# Start the trunk...)**. Then he saw *zap!* with no explanation. His eyes narrowed slightly. What was this? An obstacle? Energy? An error? The lack of a comment made it ambiguous.

He decided to proceed with the tree, building above the trunk, perhaps ignoring or working around the mysterious 'zap!'. He added the leafy top.

```
print ("--------------------") # Draw the ground line for our park scene
print ("      ||        ") # Start the trunk of the tree in the middle
print ("     *zap! *     ")
print ("    /-----\     ") # Canopy shelters the quiet earth
print ("   /-------\    ") # Branches reach, silent patterns
```

He added two lines for the top, and his comments were concise, almost poetic. "Alpha team sequence complete," he stated softly.

M.I.A. displayed Team Alpha's final code and the resulting text picture. The ground was there, the trunk was there, a nice leafy top was there... but right between the trunk and the leaves was a random *zap!*.

```
--------------------
      ||
     *zap!*
    /-----\
```

```
/-------\
```

Huh," Ade said, looking at the picture. "What's the zap?

Jayden sheepishly raised his hand. "Uh, that was me. I kinda forgot the comment."

Mei-Ling frowned slightly. "Without the comment, Kenji couldn't know your intention. It disrupts the visual logic of the tree."

Kenji simply observed the result, a silent lesson learned about ambiguity.

"An excellent demonstration of why comments matter," M.I.A. noted calmly, without blame. "Now, let's see Team Beta. Sofia, you begin for the friendly robot."

Team Beta - Turn 1: Sofia

Sofia wanted her robot to be cheerful right away. She decided to start with a happy head or maybe a bright light.

```
print ("   (^_^)   ") # A friendly face to start our robot friend!
```

She added a little smiley emoji to her comment for extra cheer. "Robot head ready! Passing to Lucas!" The code appeared on Lucas's board.

Team Beta - Turn 2: Lucas

Lucas analyzed Sofia's line and comment **(# A friendly face...)**. Objective: Construct robot body below the head. He designed a simple, functional torso.

```
print ("   (^_^)   ") # A friendly face to start our robot friend!
print ("    / [___]\     ") # Main chassis unit, housing core components.
```

His comment was precise, like an engineering note. "Chassis assembly complete. Transferring code to Samira."

Team Beta - Turn 3: Samira

Samira saw the happy head **(# A friendly face...)** and the sturdy body **(# Main chassis unit...).** The robot needed to stand or move. She decided on simple legs, but her comment added a layer of thought.

```
print("   (^_^)   ") # A friendly face to start our robot friend!
print("  /[___]\  ") # Main chassis unit, housing core components.
print("   || ||   ") # Adding legs for stability. # Does mobility imply freedom?
```

She added two comments – one explaining the code, the other posing a thoughtful question inspired by the act of creation. "Robot grounded," she said quietly. "Team Beta sequence complete."

M.I.A. displayed Team Beta's final code and picture:

```
  (^_^)
 /[___]\
  || ||
```

A cute, simple robot stood there.

"Aww, he's cute!" Sofia clapped lightly.

Lucas nodded. "Logical construction sequence followed. Comments provided necessary context for component integration."

Samira looked at their creation. "It feels... complete. We understood what the others were adding because of the comments."

M.I.A. let both final pictures hang in the air for comparison. Team Alpha's tree had a mysterious, uncommented *zap!* interrupting its form. Team Beta's robot looked coherent and cheerful, each part logically following the last, guided by explanatory comments.

"See the difference?" M.I.A. asked gently. "Both teams used the same print() command. Both added lines sequentially. But

Team Beta's consistent use of comments allowed for smoother collaboration and a clearer final result. Jayden's missed comment on Team Alpha, while unintentional, created confusion for Kenji."

Jayden rubbed the back of his neck. "Yeah, my bad. I see how just typing # Added cool stuff wouldn't have helped much either. You gotta say *what* it is."

"Exactly," Ade agreed. "The comment connects your idea to the next person's." He thought for a moment, then added, looking at his own comment, "Maybe signing off is good too? Like 'Passing to Mei-Ling! - Ade'."

Sofia lit up. "Ooh! And we could add little encouraging notes! Like, # Great start, Sofia! Adding the body now. - Lucas."

Lucas considered this. "While potentially superfluous from a purely technical documentation standpoint, positive reinforcement could enhance team morale and collaborative synergy." He gave a small nod. "Acceptable."

Samira looked at her own comment again. **# Does mobility imply freedom? "**And comments can be for more than just explaining *what* the code does," she mused. "They can be for asking questions, thinking about the impact, or suggesting improvements."

Kenji spoke softly, looking at his own poetic comments on Team Alpha's code. **"# Branches reach, silent patterns."** He added, "Code tells machine. Comment tells mind. Sometimes... tells heart."

Mei-Ling's eyes gained a thoughtful distance. "If comments help us understand code now... could we use them to leave messages for people who use our code *later*? Or even... for other students in Class Infinity, maybe years from now, who might look at our old projects?"

M.I.A.'s light seemed to glow a little brighter. "An exceptionally insightful idea, Mei-Ling. Code is often built upon layers created by many people over time. Leaving clear comments is like leaving a helpful guide for future explorers, ensuring your work can be understood, built upon, and improved."

"So, comments aren't just chores," Ade summarized. "They're like... part of being a good coder citizen? Helping others understand."

"They are a fundamental part of responsible and collaborative programming," M.I.A. confirmed. "They help with debugging, teamwork, maintenance, and ensuring that the *human* element – the *why* behind the code – isn't lost."

The kids looked at their Code Boards, no longer seeing just tools for typing commands, but interfaces for communication – with the Nexus, and with each other. The simple # symbol held a new weight, a new importance.

They had learned to print, learned the power of sequence, and now learned the vital role of communication through comments. Each step built upon the last, revealing more about the thoughtful process behind building with code. It wasn't just about making things work; it was about making things understandable, shareable, and maintainable. It was about thinking like part of a team, even if that team included their own future selves.

M.I.A. surveyed the seven students, a sense of progress filling the luminous space of the Nexus. They were absorbing not just the syntax, but the *culture* of coding – the practices that separated functional code from truly useful, collaborative code.

"You've learned to speak to the machine with print()," M.I.A. recapped. "You've learned the importance of order with sequence. And today, you've learned to speak to each other, through time and distance, using comments (#)."

The AI paused, letting the significance of this communication channel sink in. The hash symbol, #, now felt like a key, unlocking a new layer of interaction within their digital world.

"Remember this," M.I.A. concluded, its voice resonating with gentle wisdom. "Code tells the computer what to do. Comments tell humans *why*."

M.I.A.'s light pulsed softly, encompassing them all.

"Every great coder writes for two minds: the computer, and another human who will read their thoughts."

CHAPTER 6: DEBUGGING DUNGEONS

The satisfying glow of M.I.A.'s final words about comments still lingered: "Every great coder writes for two minds: the computer, and another human who will read their thoughts." Ade felt a sense of accomplishment. They were learning not just commands, but how to think, how to sequence, how to communicate through code. It felt... important.

"You are learning the foundations," M.I.A.'s voice resonated through the Infinity Nexus, pulling Ade from his thoughts. "You know how to give instructions using print(). You understand that the *order* of those instructions, the sequence, is crucial. And you know how to leave messages for yourselves and others using comments #."

M.I.A. paused, its light form pulsing gently. "But what happens when, despite your best efforts, your instructions... don't work?"

Jayden groaned dramatically. "Oh no, not another party disaster!"

M.I.A. chimed softly, a sound like digital laughter. "Not exactly a party, Jayden. But building anything, whether with code or blocks or ideas, sometimes involves things going wrong. Instructions can be misunderstood, rules accidentally broken. In programming, we call these mistakes **bugs**."

"Like the syntax errors we saw before?" Mei-Ling asked, already reaching for the virtual notepad she'd started imagining.

"Syntax errors are one type of bug," M.I.A. confirmed. "Mistakes in the language's grammar. But there are others. Today, you will face these bugs head-on. You will learn the essential skill of **debugging** – finding and fixing errors in your code."

Sofia shifted nervously in her circle. "Fixing errors? Does that mean we did something wrong?"

"It means you are learning!" M.I.A. corrected warmly. "Every single person who writes code makes mistakes. Experts make mistakes. The creators of the most complex systems make mistakes. Bugs are not failures; they are puzzles. Debugging is the process of solving those puzzles. And it's one of the most important skills you can learn."

M.I.A. gestured, and the familiar, vast platform around them began to change. The distant libraries and floating screens faded, replaced by something new. Glowing walls of light, like intricate circuit boards brought to life, rose around them, forming twisting pathways. The air hummed with a low, challenging energy.

"Whoa! Where are we now?" Jayden breathed, eyes wide as the environment shifted into a luminous labyrinth. The walls pulsed with soft colours – blues, greens, purples – and occasionally flickered, as if rearranging themselves.

"Welcome," M.I.A. announced, its voice echoing slightly in the new space, "to the **Debugging Dungeon**."

The name sounded slightly ominous, but the place itself felt more intriguing than scary. It was like stepping inside a giant, beautiful, ever-changing puzzle box.

In front of each student, hovering just above the glowing floor, a small, creature made of pure white light appeared. It looked like a simple, rounded robot, about the size of a football, with two little light-stub legs. It pulsed with a steady, ready glow.

"These are your **CodeBots**," M.I.A. explained. "Your task is simple: guide your CodeBot through a section of the Debugging Dungeon maze using only print() commands."

"Just print()?" Lucas asked. "How does printing text guide a physical bot?"

"A perceptive question, Lucas," M.I.A. replied. "Think of it this way: certain printed messages are 'magic words' the bot understands as commands. For this challenge, print("forward") tells the bot to move one step forward, print("left") tells it to turn left, and print("right") tells it to turn right. Your goal is to give it the correct sequence of commands to reach the glowing exit portal at the end of your path."

It sounded straightforward enough. Use **print()** to give move commands. They knew print(). They knew sequence.

"But," M.I.A. added, a subtle change in its tone, "there's a catch. Before you arrived, tiny gremlins – bugs! – crept into your Code Boards. Each of you has a small error hiding in the simple sequence of commands I've pre-loaded for you. Your bot won't move correctly until you find and fix your specific bug."

A collective "Oh..." went through the group.

"Your Code Boards now show your starting sequence," M.I.A. instructed. "Examine it, then try to run it. Observe what happens. The Dungeon, and your bot, will give you clues."

Ade looked down at his Code Board. A few lines of code glowed there

```
# Instructions for my CodeBot
print("forward")
print("left")
print("forward" # Missing closing quote here?
print("right")
```

Self-correction during thought: The prompt said pre-set bugs, so the comment shouldn't give it away. I'll remove that comment.

Revised code on Ade's board:

```
# Instructions for my CodeBot
print("forward")
print("left")
print("forward
print("right")
```

Hmm, that's not quite right either, a missing quote usually flags differently. Let's give Ade the missing closing parenthesis.

Corrected pre-set bug for Ade:

```
# Instructions for my CodeBot
print("forward")
print("left")
print("forward") # Let's assume this line is correct
print("right"  # Missing closing parenthesis
```

Okay, that works.

Sofia looked at her board:

```
# My Robot's Happy Path
print("forward")
print(forward") # Missing opening quote
print("left")
```

Lucas examined his:

```
# Bot Motion Sequence v1.0
```

print("forward") # Unexpected indent

print("right")

print("forward")

Jayden glanced at his:

 # Go Go Bot!

print("left")

print("forward" # Missing closing parenthesis

print("forward")

Self-correction: Ade already has missing parenthesis. Let's give Jayden a typo in print.

Revised pre-set bug for Jayden:

 # Go Go Bot!

prnit("left") # Typo in 'print'

print("forward")

print("forward")

Much better.

Mei-Ling studied hers:

 # Sequence Log Alpha

print("right")

print("forward")

print("left" # **Missing closing parenthesis**

Self-correction: Ade and Jayden have parenthesis/typo issues. Let's give Mei-Ling a missing closing quote.

Revised pre-set bug for Mei-Ling:

 # Sequence Log Alpha

print("right")

print("forward")

print("left) **# Missing closing quote**

Samira read hers:

 # Guiding Light Bot

print("forward")

print("forward")

print("right") **# Let's make this one more subtle - maybe** extra quote?

print("right""") **# Extra quote**

Okay, an extra quote.

Kenji observed his:

 # Path Protocol

print("forward")

print(("left")) **# Double parentheses**

print("forward")

Double parentheses - that's a good subtle one.

"Alright," M.I.A. said, "When you're ready, try running your code. Let the debugging begin!"

Jayden, never one for patience, immediately hit 'Enter' on his Code Board. His little CodeBot pulsed... then fizzled with a sad little *bzzzt* sound, refusing to move. Red error text flashed onto his Code Board:

NameError on line 1: name 'prnit' is not defined.

"What?! 'Prnit'?" Jayden yelled, throwing his hands up in the air (carefully avoiding the Code Board). "'Name Error'? It's not a name, it's a command! Stupid bot!" He kicked the air in frustration.

Sofia nervously tapped 'Enter'. Her CodeBot jolted, spun in a circle emitting confused little sparks, and then bumped gently into the glowing wall beside it. Her board flashed:

SyntaxError on line 2: invalid syntax. Perhaps you forgot a comma or a quote?

"Oh no!" Sofia gasped, her eyes welling up slightly. "It crashed! I broke it! What did I do?" She looked desperately at M.I.A., her lower lip trembling.

M.I.A. glided slightly closer to Sofia, its light soft and reassuring. "Breathe, Sofia. You didn't break anything permanently. The bot simply couldn't understand the instruction because of a small syntax error. That's okay! The error message is a clue. It even suggests checking for quotes."

M.I.A. then addressed everyone. "Do not panic when you see an error! It's the Dungeon's way of talking back, telling you *where* it got confused. Look at the line number. Read the message. Compare it to the rules you know."

Sofia took a deep breath, looking again at her code and the message. Line 2... quotes... print(forward"). Wait...

Meanwhile, Lucas ran his code. His bot didn't even move. It just sat there, and his board showed:

IndentationError on line 1: unexpected indent.

Lucas frowned, adjusting his glasses. "IndentationError... Line 1..." He examined print("forward"). "Ah. An extraneous leading space character. Python is sensitive to whitespace at the beginning of lines. Logical." He calmly deleted the extra space before print.

He ran it again. This time, the bot beeped happily and moved forward one step into the maze! "Error resolved. Proceeding to next instruction block," he stated methodically.

Mei-Ling ran her code. Her bot shuddered and stopped.
SyntaxError on line 3: EOL while scanning string literal.

"EOL?" she murmured. "End Of Line... while scanning string literal." She looked at Line 3: print("left). "A string literal is the text inside quotes," she reasoned. "If it reached the end of the line while still scanning the string... it must mean the string never officially ended." She tapped her virtual notepad. "Hypothesis: Missing closing quotation mark."

She carefully added the " after left. print("left"). She ran the code. *Beep!* The bot executed the sequence: right, forward, left. Success! "Hypothesis confirmed. Bug remediated," she noted.

Ade watched Lucas and Mei-Ling succeed, feeling encouraged. He ran his code:

```
    # Instructions for my CodeBot
print("forward")
print("left")
print("forward")
print("right"  # Missing closing parenthesis
```

His bot moved forward, turned left, moved forward again... then sputtered and froze before the last turn. His board showed:

SyntaxError on line 4: unexpected EOF while parsing.

"EOF... End Of File?" Ade puzzled. "Line 4... print("right"... It reached the end of the entire code file while trying to understand that line?" He remembered M.I.A.'s emphasis on syntax. print needs (). Text needs "". His line had print("right". He was missing the closing). "Ah!" He added the parenthesis: print("right"). He ran it again. *Beep!* Forward, left, forward, right! His bot reached its first checkpoint. He grinned. "Got it!"

Kenji ran his code:

```
    # Path Protocol
print("forward")
print(("left")) # Double parentheses
print("forward")
```

His bot moved forward, turned left, moved forward. It worked! No error message flashed. But the bot stopped *before* the designated exit portal for his section. M.I.A.'s voice gently prompted, "Check the expected path, Kenji. Did the bot follow all intended turns?"

Kenji observed the bot's position relative to the glowing exit. It seemed one step short. He reviewed his code. print(("left")). While technically not always a syntax error depending on context, the *double* parentheses were unusual. He suspected the Dungeon's 'magic word' system might be strict. He simplified it to the standard print("left"). He ran it again. Forward, left, forward. The bot reached the portal perfectly. He nodded. Redundancy removed. Clarity improved.

Samira ran her code:

```
# Guiding Light Bot
print("forward")
print("forward")
print("right""") # Extra quote
```

Her bot moved forward twice, then jittered violently and faded slightly, stopping dead. The error message appeared:

SyntaxError on line 3: EOL while scanning string literal. (Or a similar syntax error depending on exact Python version's parsing of triple quotes).

"End of line... string literal..." Samira murmured, reading Mei-Ling's earlier conclusion. She looked closely at line 3: print("right"""). "Three quotes?" she wondered. "Maybe it thinks the string ends after the second quote, and the third one is... extra? Confusing?" She carefully deleted the final quote: print("right"). She ran the code. *Beep!* Forward, forward, right. The bot smoothly reached its destination. She smiled softly. "Less confusion is better."

Only Jayden was left, still fuming at his Code Board. "NameError! How can prnit be a name error? It's obviously supposed to be print!"

Ade, having finished his section, noticed Jayden's struggle. "Hey Jayden," he called over gently. "Remember what M.I.A. said? The computer is super literal. It doesn't know what you *meant* to type, only what you *did* type."

Jayden glared at his board. prnit. He looked closer. P... R... N... I... T. "Oh." His shoulders slumped. "I swapped the 'n' and 'i'." He felt a flush of embarrassment. Such a small mistake had caused so much frustration. Slowly, carefully, he corrected the typo: print("left"). He took a deep breath and ran the code.

Beep! Left, forward, forward. His CodeBot zoomed through its path and reached the exit.

"YES!" Jayden shouted, relief washing over him. "Okay, okay! Typos. Gotta watch the typos! Slow down..." He actually grinned. Finding the bug felt almost as good as getting it right the first time.

One by one, they navigated their initial sections, fixing their unique bugs. Lucas methodically removed his indent. Mei-Ling closed her quote. Ade added his parenthesis. Sofia found her missing opening quote ("Oh! There it is! Silly me!"). Kenji streamlined his parentheses. Samira removed her extra quote. And Jayden conquered his typo.

The maze walls shifted slightly, revealing new paths and new code sequences on their boards, each with another subtle bug waiting.

They continued, section by section. Sometimes the errors were simple typos again. Sometimes they forgot a # and accidentally tried to run a comment. Sometimes they mixed up "left" and "right", which wasn't a syntax error, but a **logic error** – the code ran, but the bot went the wrong way.

When a bot went off course due to a logic error, M.I.A. would gently ask, "The code ran correctly, but did the bot follow the path you *intended*? Check your instructions against the maze map."

This required a different kind of debugging – tracing the steps, comparing the intended path to the actual commands.

Frustration still flared, especially for Jayden when he made a repeat mistake. Sofia still needed occasional deep breaths when her bot crashed unexpectedly. But they were learning.

They learned to read the error messages carefully – SyntaxError, NameError, IndentationError became familiar clues, not scary accusations.
They learned to check the line number indicated in the error.
They learned to compare their code, character by character, against the correct syntax: print("text").
They learned to test changes one at a time.
They learned, as Lucas pointed out, that "Systematic elimination of possibilities is key."

They also started helping each other more. Ade patiently explained the EOF error to Sofia when she encountered it later. Kenji, after fixing his own logic error, noticed Samira's bot turning left into a wall. He subtly typed a comment on his *own* board that only M.I.A. relayed visually near Samira: # Path requires right turn at glowing junction. Verify command. Samira saw it, checked her code, and found her print("left") where a print("right") should have been. She smiled gratefully towards Kenji.

Mei-Ling kept meticulous notes on her virtual pad: "Attempt 3: Line 5, added missing ')', Result: Success." It helped her track what worked and what didn't.

Samira, watching her bot finally navigate a tricky section after she fixed a logic bug, had a thought. *It feels good to fix something broken,* she reflected. *To understand why it failed and guide it back to the right path. Maybe debugging isn't just about code... maybe it's about patience, and not giving up on things – or people – when they don't work perfectly right away.*

Finally, after navigating several challenging sections, fixing syntax errors and logic bugs, guiding their beeping, glowing

CodeBots through the shifting maze, they all reached a large, open chamber at the end of the Dungeon.

The walls here were calmer, glowing with a soft, warm light. Floating gently in the air were holographic displays, like museum exhibits.

"Congratulations, Voyagers," M.I.A. announced, its voice filled with warmth. "You have successfully navigated the Debugging Dungeon."

A cheer went up from the group, relief mixing with pride.

"Look around you," M.I.A. invited. "This is the **Bug Zoo**."

Each display case seemed to contain... a bug? Not real insects, but shimmering, holographic representations of the errors they had just faced. One showed a tangled knot labelled SyntaxError: Mismatched Quotes. Another showed a blocky character tripping over a space labelled IndentationError. A third showed a word dissolving, labelled NameError: Typo Detected.

"This is a place to remember, and even celebrate, the bugs you find and fix," M.I.A. explained. "Because each bug teaches you something valuable. Now, as your final step today, I want each of you to contribute to the Zoo. Think about the bug that challenged you the most, or the lesson you learned. Use your Code Board to 'add' it to an empty display."

One by one, they approached the empty holographic frames.

Jayden typed: # Bug: NameError from 'prnit'. Lesson: Slow down and check spelling! Typos happen! A display lit up with his note and a dissolving 'prnit'.

Sofia typed: # Bug: SyntaxError, missing quote. Lesson: Don't panic! Read the error message, it helps! Breathe. □ Her display showed a quote mark floating away, surrounded by sparkles.

Lucas typed: # Bug: IndentationError. Lesson: Python mandates strict indentation. Precision is paramount. His display showed a blocky character neatly aligning itself.

Mei-Ling typed: # Bug: SyntaxError, missing closing quote. Lesson: Verify string literal termination. Systematic checking prevents recurrence. Her display showed a perfectly closed quote symbol.

Ade typed: # Bug: SyntaxError, missing parenthesis. Lesson: Check every symbol matches the rules. Patience helps! His display showed a) clicking into place.

Samira typed: # Bug: Logic Error (wrong turn). Lesson: Code can be 'correct' but still wrong for the goal. Check intention. Fixing takes patience. Her display showed a little bot thoughtfully choosing between two paths.

Kenji typed: # Bug: Redundant syntax (double parenthesis). Lesson: Clarity surpasses complexity. Simple path often best. # Listen. His display showed two parentheses merging into one, with the word 'Listen' below it.

They stood back, looking at their contributions glowing in the Bug Zoo. It didn't feel like a wall of shame; it felt like a gallery of learning, a testament to their persistence. They hadn't been defeated by the errors; they had learned from them.

"You see?" M.I.A. said softly. "Errors are not endings. They are beginnings. Opportunities to understand more deeply, to think more clearly, to become better problem-solvers."

The Debugging Dungeon, once seemingly intimidating, now felt like a valuable training ground. They had faced the frustration of failure and found the satisfaction of fixing it themselves.

M.I.A.'s light pulsed with encouragement, reflecting in the holographic displays of the Bug Zoo.

"Every error is a clue," the AI stated, its voice resonating with the core lesson of the day. "Every clue brings you closer to mastery."

M.I.A. paused, letting them absorb the feeling of accomplishment, the new confidence gained from overcoming challenges.

"You are learning to listen to the machine," M.I.A. concluded. "And soon, you will learn how to make it listen even more effectively to you"

CHAPTER 7: MESSAGES THAT MATTER

The glowing holographic exhibits of the Bug Zoo faded behind them as the familiar, vast expanse of the main Infinity Nexus platform reformed around the seven students. The slight tension of debugging dissolved, replaced by a quiet sense of pride. They hadn't just followed instructions; they had fixed them. They had wrestled with errors and won.

Ade flexed his fingers, the phantom feel of the Code Board still tingling. Fixing that missing parenthesis error had felt surprisingly good.

"Well done, Voyagers," M.I.A.'s voice echoed, warm and approving. "You faced the bugs, deciphered their clues, and emerged victorious. Debugging is a journey of patience and precision, and you navigated it admirably."

Jayden puffed out his chest slightly. "Yeah, that 'prnit' bug won't get me again! Slow down, check the spelling. Got it."

"Indeed," M.I.A. agreed. "You are learning the foundational skills: giving instructions with print(), ensuring the correct sequence, leaving clear comments with #, and now, debugging errors when they arise. But code isn't just about making things work correctly."

M.I.A.'s light form seemed to glow a little brighter, shifting from informative guide to inspiring muse. "Code can also be a way to express yourself. To share ideas, feelings, and creativity."

Sofia's eyes widened slightly. "Express feelings? With print()?"

"Think about it," M.I.A. prompted gently. "Words express feelings. Art expresses feelings. Music expresses feelings. Code, at its heart, is a language. And language can be used for function *and* for expression."

M.I.A. paused, letting the idea settle in the luminous space. "Today, we explore how even the simple print() command can become a paintbrush, a sculptor's chisel, a writer's pen. We will learn how to shape your messages, make them span multiple lines, and create visual designs using text."

Lucas adjusted his glasses. "Are you referring to multi-line string literals or the use of newline escape characters within standard string declarations?"

M.I.A. chimed softly. "Both are possibilities, Lucas! Python offers tools for structure. One simple way is using triple quotes."

Three quote marks appeared beside M.I.A.: """

"When you start and end a block of text with three quotation marks – either double """ or single ''' – Python understands that everything in between, including line breaks you type, is part of one single message," M.I.A. explained.

An example glowed:

```
    print("""
This message
will appear
on multiple lines,
exactly as typed!
""")
```

"This is wonderful for poems, addresses, or creating simple pictures with text – often called **ASCII art**," M.I.A. added.

Ade thought about the little text cake Lucas had made. That must have used separate print() lines. But this triple-quote thing could make bigger pictures easier.

"The other way, as Lucas alluded to," M.I.A. continued, "is using a special code inside regular quotes: \n."

The symbol \n glowed.

"This doesn't print literally," M.I.A. explained. "Instead, \n tells Python: 'Start a new line here.' It's called the **newline character**."

Another example:

```
print("Hello!\nWelcome to the Nexus.\nIsn't coding fun?")
```

M.I.A. showed the output:

Hello!

Welcome to the Nexus.

Isn't coding fun?

"Two tools," M.I.A. summarized. "Triple quotes for easy blocks, \n for precise newlines within strings. Both let you control the shape and flow of your text output."

The AI turned its glowing attention to the students, its voice filled with gentle encouragement. "Now, for your next challenge. I want you to use these tools, along with careful spacing and alignment, to create a personal message. Something that reflects *you*."

M.I.A. paused, letting the weight of the invitation sink in.

"It could be a motto you believe in. A picture representing something you love. A greeting that shares your personality. A quote that inspires you."

The AI's light pulsed softly. "Think of it this way: **Code can be a**

mirror. What you write reflects what you care about."

"Your task is to design and code this personal 'Message That Matters' using print(), multi-line techniques, spacing, and maybe even comments to explain your creation. Take your time. Experiment. Make it yours."

A quiet excitement filled the Nexus. This wasn't about fixing errors or following strict steps for a group project. This was personal. This was creative. What would they make?

Sofia's Creation: Whispers of Nature

Sofia immediately thought of the rainforests back home in Brazil. The vibrant colours, the chirping birds, the feeling of life teeming everywhere. She wanted to capture a sense of that, a plea for its protection. Animation with print() seemed hard, but maybe she could imply movement?

She started sketching ideas on her Code Board, using symbols and emojis within triple quotes.

```
print("""
   □□□
 / O \_/ O \
| □ >-(_)-< □ | # Little friends in the canopy!
 \___/ \___/
     | |
   /-----\
  /-------\ □ # Life needs water!
 ~~~~~~~~~~~~~  <-- The gentle river flows...
""")
```

She frowned. It was static. How to make it feel more alive? Maybe... print several frames? She tried printing a tree, then using empty print() lines to create space (like clearing the screen visually in the Nexus), then printing a slightly different tree with a bird () appearing.

 # Frame 1: Quiet Forest

```
print("""
      □ □
   / \_/ \
  |       |
   \___/ \___/
      | |
    /-----\
   /-------\
  ~~~~~~~~~~~~
""")
print("\n" * 5) # Add spacing for next 'frame'

# Frame 2: Bird Appears!
print("""
      □□□
   / O \_/ O \
  | □     | # A colourful bird arrives!
   \___/ \___/
    | |
   /-----\
  /-------\ □
 ~~~~~~~~~~~~
""")
```

She ran it. The first tree appeared in her signature shimmering pink, then faded slightly as the second one appeared below it, the little blue bird emoji adding a touch of life. It wasn't true animation, but it felt like a small story unfolding. She added a final message below it: print("Protect our beautiful world! "). Perfect.

Jayden's Creation: The Joke-a-Tron 3000

Jayden loved making people laugh. His mission: a scrolling joke board! He decided to use sequential print() calls with empty print()s in between to create a sense of timing, like a stand-up comedian.

```
# JOKE-A-TRON 3000 - Prepare for Laughter!
print("*********************")
print("*  JOKE-A-TRON   *")
print("*    3000      *")
print("*********************")
print() # Pause for effect
print("Why don't scientists trust atoms?")
print()
print()
print("...") # Dramatic pause...
print()
print("Because they make up everything!")
print("□□□") # Laugh track!
print("\n" * 3) # Space before next joke

# Joke 2
print("What do you call a lazy kangaroo?")
print()
```

```
print("...")
print()
print("Pouch potato!")
print("□")
print("--- END TRANSMISSION ---")
```

He ran it. The title card appeared in flashing green, then the first joke unfolded with pauses, followed by the second. It felt interactive, punchy. "Yes! Digital comedy gold!" he declared, already thinking of more jokes to add later.

Ade's Creation: An Invitation to Infinity

Ade thought about why he loved tinkering, why technology fascinated him. It was about potential, about unlocking possibilities within himself and others. He wanted his message to be welcoming, inspiring. He remembered the name of their class: Class Infinity.

He decided on a clear, centered message using triple quotes for structure and careful spacing.

```
# Welcome message - inspired by Class Infinity
print("""
+----------------------------------------+
|                     |
|   Welcome, Curious Mind!          |
|                     |
| Every mind is Infinity waiting      |
| to be unlocked.             |
|                     |
|   Let's explore together.         |
|                     |
```

```
+--------------------------------------+
""")
print() # Add a little space below
print("# Stay curious! - Ade") # Personal sign-off in a comment
```

He ran the code. The message appeared in his steady blue, framed by a neat box made of text characters. It felt solid, hopeful, and open. He liked how the comment added a personal touch without being part of the main display.

Mei-Ling's Creation: Echoes of Home

Mei-Ling valued family and heritage. She decided to write her family name, '王' (Wang), which means 'king', in a way that suggested tradition and elegance. She thought about calligraphy, the flow of ink. Could she mimic that with text? She decided to use sequential print() commands with increasing indentation to create a cascading effect.

```
# Displaying the family name 'Wang' (王) with cascading style
print("    王")
print() # Small vertical space
print("     王")
print()
print("      王")
print()
print("       王")
print("\n# Echoing generations. - Mei-Ling")
```

She ran it. The character '王' appeared four times in her precise orange, each one slightly lower and further to the right, like steps descending or echoes fading. It was simple, yet held a quiet dignity. She added the comment to explain the feeling behind it.

Samira's Creation: A Code for Kindness

Samira often thought about fairness, about how people treated each other. She wanted her message to reflect the importance of empathy and justice in any world, digital or physical. She chose a quote that resonated with her and used triple quotes to format it thoughtfully.

```
    # A message about how we build our world
```

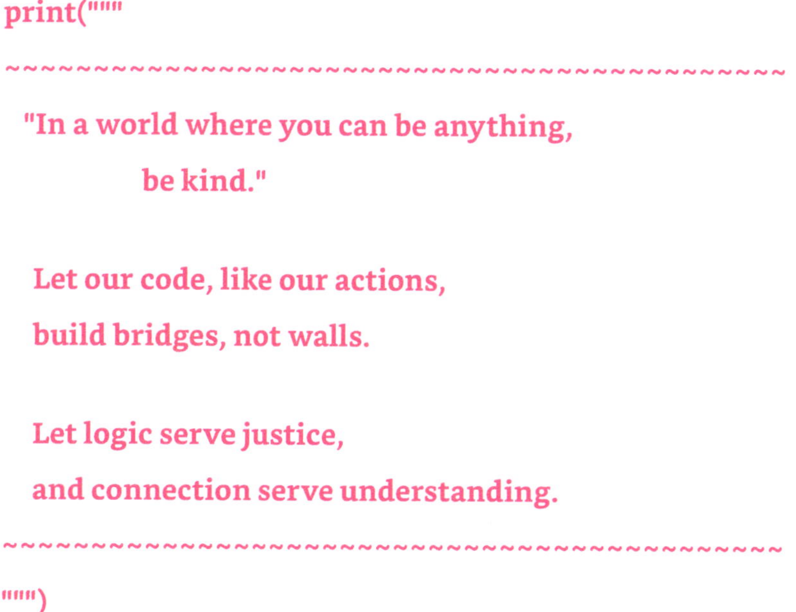

```
print("""
~~~~~~~~~~~~~~~~~~~~~~~~~~~~~~~~~~~~~~~~~~~~
  "In a world where you can be anything,
            be kind."

  Let our code, like our actions,
  build bridges, not walls.

  Let logic serve justice,
  and connection serve understanding.
~~~~~~~~~~~~~~~~~~~~~~~~~~~~~~~~~~~~~~~~~~~~
""")
print("# Think ethically, act kindly. - Samira")
```

She executed the code. The message appeared in her calm cyan, framed by gentle wavy lines. The core quote stood out, supported by her own reflections on coding's role. The final comment was a reminder to herself as much as anyone else.

Kenji's Creation: The Point of Stillness

Kenji valued focus, observation, and finding clarity in simplicity. He didn't need many words. He decided on a single word, perfectly centered, presented with stark symmetry. He spent time calculating the exact spaces needed before the word on his Code

Board.

```
# Centered focus point
print()
print()
print("          +---------------+          ")
print("          |               |          ")
print("          |    Observe    |          ")
print("          |               |          ")
print("          +---------------+          ")
print()
print("# Stillness reveals. - Kenji")
```

He ran the code. In his deep indigo, the word "Observe" appeared, perfectly suspended within a minimalist box, surrounded by empty space. It felt powerful in its quiet intensity. A single point of focus in the vast Nexus. The comment added a layer of Zen-like interpretation.

Lucas's Creation: Logic Matrix

Lucas saw beauty in structure, data, and the underlying logic of systems. He decided to create a visual representation of this. He envisioned a grid, like a data matrix, where the pattern itself formed a message. He used many print() lines, carefully placing characters.

```
# Data Matrix forming "Logic is Light"
print("L 0 G 1 C 0 1 0 I S 0 L 1 G H T")
print("0 # 1 # 0 # 1 # 0 # 1 # 0 # 1 #")
print("L 0 G 1 C 0 1 0 I S 0 L 1 G H T")
print("1 # 0 # 1 # 0 # 1 # 0 # 1 # 0 #")
print("L 0 G 1 C 0 1 0 I S 0 L 1 G H T")
```

```
print("0 # 1 # 0 # 1 # 0 # 1 # 0 # 1 #")
print("# Data pattern encodes message. - Lucas")
```

He executed the commands. A grid of letters, numbers, and hash symbols appeared in his sharp white text. At first glance, it looked like random data, but reading horizontally revealed the repeating phrase "L 0 G 1 C 0 1 0 I S 0 L 1 G H T". Within the structure, the message "Logic is Light" was embedded. He nodded, satisfied with the efficient encoding of concept within form.

M.I.A. glided silently around the platform as each student finished their creation. The AI paused by each glowing text display, its light seeming to absorb the unique expression before it. No critiques, just quiet appreciation.

Sofia's gentle nature scene flickered beside Jayden's energetic joke board. Ade's welcoming message stood near Mei-Ling's elegant family name cascade. Samira's thoughtful words on kindness contrasted with Kenji's stark call to observe, while Lucas's logic matrix pulsed nearby.

The Nexus felt vibrant, filled with their distinct personalities rendered in code.

"Wow, Sofia, yours is so pretty!" Ade exclaimed, admiring the implied animation of her forest scene. "How did you make the bird appear later?"

"I just printed the first picture, then used empty print() lines like print('\\n' * 5) to make space, then printed the second picture!" Sofia explained happily. "It's like flipping pages!"

Jayden laughed at his own joke output. "Lucas, yours looks like something out of a sci-fi movie! Took me a second to see the words!"

Lucas nodded. "The objective was pattern-based information embedding. The aesthetic is secondary, though not unwelcome."

Mei-Ling studied Kenji's centered "Observe". "The spacing is perfect, Kenji. Very precise. It draws the eye."

Kenji gave a slight nod towards Mei-Ling's cascading name. "Flow. Elegant."

Samira looked thoughtfully at Ade's message. "'Every mind is Infinity waiting to be unlocked.' That really fits this place, Ade. It feels welcoming."

Ade smiled. "Thanks, Samira. Yours made me think too. About using code for good things."

They noticed how different their approaches were, even using the same simple print() command. Sofia used symbols and implied motion. Jayden focused on timing and humour. Ade aimed for inspiration and structure. Mei-Ling sought elegance and heritage. Samira focused on ethics and meaning. Kenji embraced minimalism and focus. Lucas built intricate patterns with data.

Their code truly was a mirror.

M.I.A. finally spoke, its voice filled with warmth that seemed to embrace all their creations. "Beautifully done, Voyagers. Each of you has used the same tool – the print() command – yet you have produced wonderfully unique expressions."

The AI turned its form slightly towards the group. "Do you see it? The structure Lucas built, the artistry Sofia found, the humour Jayden shared, the heritage Mei-Ling honoured, the ideals Samira expressed, the focus Kenji embodied, the welcome Ade offered. Your code carries your signature."

They looked at their glowing text messages again, seeing them now not just as exercises, but as extensions of themselves. It was a powerful feeling – shaping technology, even in this simple way, to reflect something personal and meaningful.

"Learning to code isn't just about learning rules and commands," M.I.A. continued. "It's about finding your voice in this new language. It's about learning how to translate your ideas, your passions, your very self into instructions a machine can understand and share."

The students felt a new layer of understanding click into place. Coding wasn't just technical; it was personal. It wasn't just logic; it was expression. The Nexus didn't just feel like a school; it felt like a studio, a workshop, a place where their inner worlds could take digital form.

They had moved from fixing things to making things, and in making things, they had revealed a part of themselves.

M.I.A. allowed the moment of reflection to linger, the seven personal messages glowing softly as testament to their individuality and newfound expressive power. The journey so far – from basic prints to sequence, comments, debugging, and now creative expression – felt like assembling a toolkit for a grand adventure.

The AI's light pulsed gently, gathering their attention for the next step.

"Your code spoke volumes today," M.I.A. affirmed, its voice resonating with pride and anticipation. "Individually, you have shown remarkable creativity and insight."

M.I.A. paused, letting the praise settle before shifting the focus. The light around the AI seemed to coalesce, hinting at a new direction.

"Now..." M.I.A.'s voice held a new spark, a call to unity.

The seven students looked up, sensing the transition. They had explored their individual voices. What came next?

"...are you ready to speak together, as a team?

CHAPTER 8: THE PACT

The Infinity Nexus hummed around them, filled with the lingering echoes of their individual 'Messages That Matter'. Sofia's sparkling forest, Jayden's scrolling jokes, Ade's welcoming sign, Mei-Ling's cascading name, Samira's call for kindness, Kenji's centered focus, Lucas's logic matrix – each creation was a distinct thread, reflecting the unique mind that wove it.

"Individually, you have found your voices in the language of code," M.I.A.'s voice resonated, warm and encompassing. "You have learned to instruct, to order, to comment, to debug, and to express. You've assembled the foundational tools."

M.I.A.'s form seemed to gather light, becoming slightly more focused, more intent. "Now, for the final challenge of this first stage of your journey. A challenge that requires not just individual skill, but collective harmony."

The seven students straightened up in their glowing circles, sensing the importance of this moment. This felt different. Bigger.

"You have worked alone, you have debugged errors, you have expressed yourselves," M.I.A. continued. "Now, you must work together. Your task is to combine all that you have learned –

print(), formatting, sequence, comments, and the lessons from debugging – to create one shared message. A digital statement, coded as a team, reflecting your values, your experience here, and your hopes as the first members of Class Infinity."

"A group message?" Ade repeated, glancing around at the others. Their styles were so different. How would they combine Sofia's art, Lucas's logic, and Jayden's jokes into one thing?

"Think of it as your Team Pact," M.I.A. suggested. "A declaration, rendered in code, that captures the spirit of your collaboration. It should incorporate different visual styles, use multi-line formatting effectively, and crucially, include comments explaining each contribution, signed with your names."

The AI paused, letting the scope of the challenge settle. "This is your first true collaborative build."

Page 4

A wave of excited, nervous energy rippled through the group. How would they even start?

"Okay, team!" Jayden burst out immediately. "It should be awesome! Like, flashing lights, maybe a cool game character made of text pops up? And a leaderboard! print('Class Infinity Rules!') really big!" He mimed explosive graphics with his hands.

Sofia frowned slightly. "Flashing lights? I was thinking something more... gentle? Like our messages weaving together? Maybe with stars or leaves?" She pictured flowing text and soft colours.

Lucas adjusted his glasses. "A structured approach is required. We should define parameters. Objective: A mission statement. Content: Key learnings and group values. Format: Logically sectioned, potentially using ASCII borders for clarity. Aesthetics are secondary to information content."

Samira nodded thoughtfully at Lucas's point but added her own focus. "And it should say something important. About using these skills responsibly? Maybe about connection, since we're from all over the world?"

Mei-Ling held up a virtual finger, ever the organizer. "We need a plan. Who writes what? How do we ensure consistency? We should outline the sections first. And mandatory commenting for each block is essential for clarity and attribution."

Kenji remained silent, observing the energetic, slightly chaotic exchange of ideas. His gaze drifted across the Nexus, as if seeing the potential form in the empty space.

Ade listened, hearing the passion in each voice but also the divergence. Jayden's energy, Sofia's artistry, Lucas's structure, Samira's ethics, Mei-Ling's organization... how could they possibly merge? He felt a familiar urge to find the common thread, the point where their ideas could meet.

"A leaderboard message isn't really us," Sofia said hesitantly to Jayden.

"But just stars and leaves might be boring!" Jayden countered, though less aggressively.

"The ethical component is crucial, but should not overshadow the core technical achievement," Lucas stated, perhaps responding to Samira.

"Structure is good, but it needs heart!" Sofia added.

The initial burst of enthusiasm was quickly turning into a tangled knot of competing visions. They looked at each other, a flicker

of uncertainty passing between them. Could they really do this together?
M.I.A.'s calm presence seemed to expand slightly, drawing their attention. "Look at each other," the AI prompted gently. "Look at the different ideas swirling between you. Is this divergence a weakness?"

The students paused, considering.

"Your different perspectives are not obstacles," M.I.A. continued, its light pulsing softly. "They are your greatest strength. Jayden brings energy. Sofia, beauty. Lucas, structure. Samira, conscience. Mei-Ling, clarity. Kenji, focus. Ade, connection."

"Don't try to force one style onto everyone," M.I.A. advised. "Instead, find the common ground. What have you all experienced here? What values have emerged for the group? Think about your journey: stepping through the portals, learning print(), facing the Debugging Dungeon, expressing yourselves."

M.I.A. gestured towards the vast Nexus around them. "What does 'Class Infinity' mean to all of you, now?"

The focus shifted. They weren't just individuals anymore; they were a group, the first students of this strange, amazing digital school.

"Learning," Ade said quietly. "We all came here to learn."

"And connection," Samira added. "Meeting each other, from different countries."

"Problem-solving," Lucas stated. "Debugging. Applying logic."

"Creativity!" Sofia chimed in. "Making things appear, expressing ideas."

"Precision," Mei-Ling offered. "Getting the details right."

"Focus," Kenji added, his single word resonating.

"And it's kinda fun!" Jayden admitted. "Like a cool challenge."

Hope, learning, connection, logic, creativity, precision, focus, challenge, fun. These were threads they all shared.

"Okay," Mei-Ling said, taking charge naturally. "Let's structure it. Maybe a header, then sections for our shared values, and a closing statement?"

Lucas nodded. "Logical. We can use ASCII borders to delineate sections."

"Could the borders have some style?" Sofia asked. "Maybe stars or waves?"

"Acceptable," Lucas conceded after a moment's thought. "Aesthetic elements can be integrated if structurally sound."

Samira spoke up. "The message about connection and using our skills well should be prominent."

Jayden tapped his chin. "Okay, okay. Maybe not flashing lights, but can we have some cool visual stuff? Like, make the words 'Class Infinity' stand out?"

"We can use spacing and perhaps different symbols around it," Mei-Ling suggested.

Kenji made a subtle gesture with his hand, mimicking careful alignment in the air. "Balance. Symmetry."

Ade saw the pieces coming together. "What if... what if the main message, the heart of it, is about the future? Like, what we're learning to build?" He paused, then offered, "Maybe a line like: 'Together, we learn to code the future.'"

There was a moment of silence as the others considered it.

"I like that," Samira said softly.

"Concise and impactful," Lucas agreed.

"It connects everything," Sofia added.

"Okay," Mei-Ling declared, pulling up her virtual notepad. "Structure proposal: Header with 'Class Infinity'. Section 1: Our Journey (learning, connection). Section 2: Our Tools (logic, creativity, precision). Section 3: Ade's line about the future. Closing: A hopeful symbol or border. Each section commented with creator names and intent."

They all nodded. It felt right. A plan forged from their combined ideas.

"Divide the canvas," M.I.A. instructed softly.

Their Code Boards seemed to link, showing a shared file, sectioned off as Mei-Ling had outlined.

"Lucas, perhaps you can frame the header and closing?" M.I.A. suggested.
"Mei-Ling, Section 1?"
"Jayden and Sofia, collaborate on Section 2 – energy and beauty?"
"Samira and Kenji, the closing symbol and ethical grounding?"
"And Ade, the central message?"

They nodded again, accepting their roles. A sense of purpose settled over them. It was time to build their Pact.

Coding - Lucas: Header & Footer

Lucas meticulously designed the top and bottom borders using characters that felt both structured and slightly expansive, like circuits reaching out.

```
# Lucas: Defining the top border structure. Precision is key.
print("+" + "=" * 50 + "+")
print("|" + " " * 50 + "|")

# ... (Code from others will go here) ...

# Lucas: Defining the bottom border, mirroring the top for balance.
print("|" + " " * 50 + "|")
print("+" + "=" * 50 + "+")
```

He ensured the width was consistent, ready for the content.

Coding - Mei-Ling: Section 1 (Journey)

Mei-Ling focused on clarity and reflecting their global origins and shared learning.

```
# Mei-Ling: Section 1 - Our shared journey begins.
print("|" + " " * 10 + "From Around the World, We Came," + " " * 9 + "|")
print("|" + " " * 10 + "Through Glowing Doors, A New Game." + " " * 8
+ "|")
print("|" + " " * 10 + "Learning Logic, Line by Line," + " " * 12 + "|")
print("|" + " " * 10 + "In Class Infinity, Our Minds Shine." + " " * 7 + "|")
print("|" + "-" * 50 + "|") # Section Divider
```

Her comments were clear, her formatting neat.

Coding - Jayden & Sofia: Section 2 (Tools)

Jayden started with energy, wanting to make 'Code' pop. Sofia refined it, adding creative symbols. They iterated, talking via comments.

```
# Jayden: Let's make CODE look awesome! POW!
# Sofia: Adding  to Jayden's energy! Let's blend logic & beauty.
print("|" + " " * 5 + "With Logic Sharp & Creative Spark " + " " * 6 + "|")
print("|" + " " * 5 + "We Debug Bugs Found in the Dark." + " " * 10 + "|")
# Jayden: Fixing a typo I made! Debugging teamwork!
print("|" + " " * 5 + "Print(), Sequence, Comments Bright," + " " * 7 +
"|")
print("|" + " " * 5 + "We Turn Ideas Into Glowing Light! " + " " * 4 + "|")
print("|" + "-" * 50 + "|") # Section Divider
```

Their combined effort balanced excitement and artistry.

Coding - Ade: Section 3 (Future)

Ade focused on centering his key line, making it stand out simply but powerfully.

```
# Ade: The core message - our shared purpose. Centered.
print("|" + " " * 50 + "|") # Blank line for emphasis
print("|" + "   Together, we learn to code the future.   " + "|")
print("|" + " " * 50 + "|") # Blank line for emphasis
print("|" + "-" * 50 + "|") # Section Divider
IGNORE_WHEN_COPYING_START
content_copy
download
Use code with caution.
Python
```

He checked the spacing carefully, wanting it to feel like the heart of their Pact.

Coding - Samira & Kenji: Closing (Ethics & Symbol)

Samira drafted the ethical reminder. Kenji designed a minimalist, hopeful symbol using text characters – perhaps a simplified globe or a rising sun – ensuring perfect alignment.

```
# Samira: A reminder of our responsibility. Connection matters.
print("|" + " " * 7 + "May Our Skills Connect and Uplift," + " " * 8 + "|")
print("|" + " " * 7 + "A Kinder World, Our Shared Gift." + " " * 9 + "|")
print("|" + " " * 50 + "|")
# Kenji: Symbol of unity and beginning. Balanced. Precise.
print("|" + " " * 21 + "---( @ )---" + " " * 20 + "|") # Simple globe/sun symbol
print("|" + " " * 21 + " / | \\ " + " " * 21 + "|")
print("|" + " " * 21 + "/___|___\\ " + " " * 20 + "|")
```

Their contributions added depth and a sense of closure.

They reviewed the complete code together on the shared board, reading through the comments, checking alignment one last time. Lucas verified structural integrity. Mei-Ling confirmed all sections were commented. Sofia admired the blend of styles. Jayden felt the contained energy. Samira saw the values reflected. Kenji nodded at the final symmetry. Ade felt a thrill of unity.

They had done it. They had woven their different threads into one tapestry of code.

"The Pact code is complete," Mei-Ling announced formally.

"Ready to run it, M.I.A.!" Jayden added eagerly.

M.I.A. seemed to gather the light in the Nexus, focusing it. "Executing Team Pact code sequence now."

A hush fell over the platform. The air crackled slightly with anticipation.

Then, it began. Line by line, the message materialized in the center of the Nexus, vastly larger than their individual creations, glowing with a composite light that blended their signature colours – Lucas's white borders framing Mei-Ling's precise orange text, flowing into Jayden's green and Sofia's pink section sparkling with yellow and cyan highlights from their emojis, leading to Ade's core message in steady blue, followed by Samira's thoughtful cyan and Kenji's deep indigo symbol, all pulsing softly together.

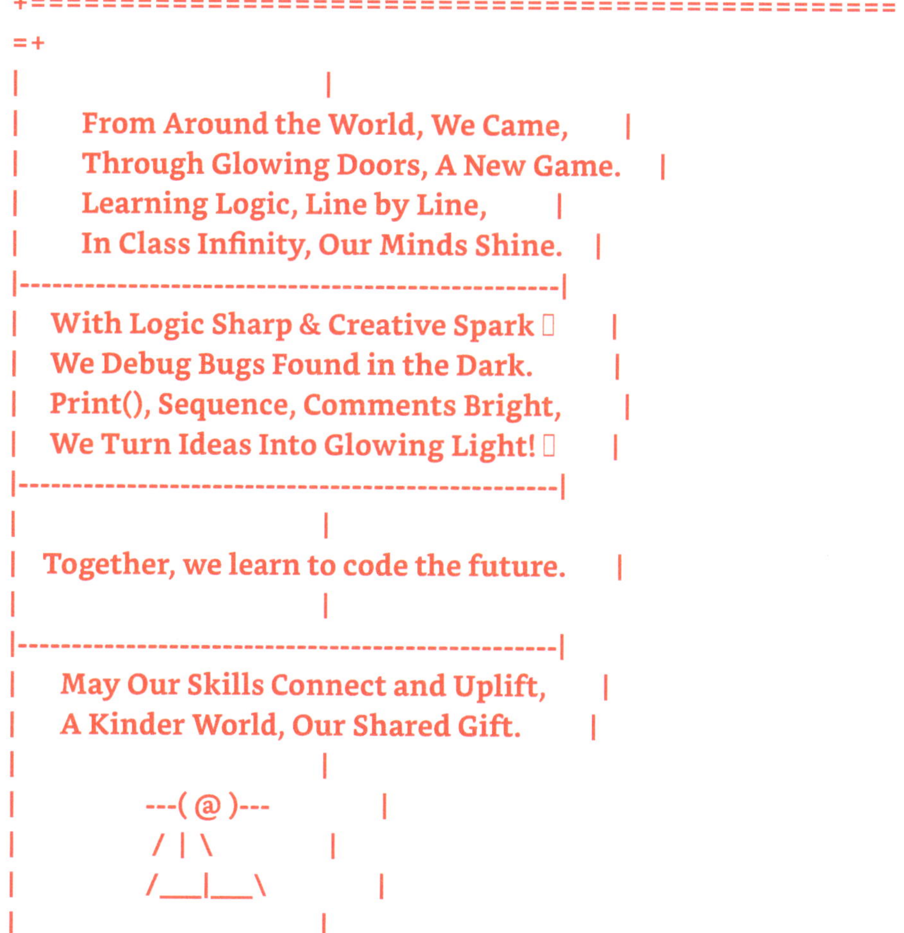

```
+==========================================
=+
|                         |
|     From Around the World, We Came,     |
|     Through Glowing Doors, A New Game.    |
|     Learning Logic, Line by Line,     |
|     In Class Infinity, Our Minds Shine.   |
|-------------------------------------------|
|   With Logic Sharp & Creative Spark □     |
|   We Debug Bugs Found in the Dark.        |
|   Print(), Sequence, Comments Bright,      |
|   We Turn Ideas Into Glowing Light! □     |
|-------------------------------------------|
|                         |
|  Together, we learn to code the future.    |
|                         |
|-------------------------------------------|
|    May Our Skills Connect and Uplift,     |
|    A Kinder World, Our Shared Gift.      |
|                         |
|          ---( @ )---          |
|           / | \          |
|          /___|___\          |
|                         |
```

+==
=+

It hung there, a magnificent digital monument woven from simple print() commands, sequence, comments, and their combined will. It was structured yet creative, logical yet hopeful, technical yet deeply personal. It was them.

"Whoa," breathed Jayden, his usual bravado replaced by genuine awe.

"It's... beautiful," Sofia whispered, tears pricking her eyes – tears of joy this time.

Lucas gave a rare, small smile. "Execution successful. Synergistic outcome achieved."

Samira felt a warmth spread through her. Seeing their shared values glowing there felt incredibly powerful. Mei-Ling nodded, satisfied with the clear, collaborative result. Kenji observed the balanced whole, a flicker of quiet pride in his eyes. Ade looked around at his teammates, then back at the glowing Pact, feeling an unbreakable bond forming between them. They weren't just seven kids anymore.

They had faced challenges alone and together. They had learned commands, logic, and the importance of communication. They had turned frustration into understanding, and simple text into meaningful expression. This glowing message was proof of their journey, a symbol of their potential.

"This Pact," M.I.A. said softly, its light reflecting off the glowing code, "represents your first completed project as a collective. It deserves to be remembered."

Seven glowing symbols, unique geometric shapes pulsing gently, appeared before each student. "Touch the symbol," M.I.A. instructed. "Commit this creation, your Team Pact, to the archives of the Nexus. Your first mark as a team."

One by one, they reached out. Ade touched his symbol, feeling a sense of shared history being made. Mei-Ling touched hers, archiving the moment of successful collaboration. Sofia touched hers, preserving the beauty they created together. Lucas touched his, logging the successful project completion. Jayden touched his, a grin replacing his earlier awe – this felt like levelling up! Samira touched hers, committing their shared values. Kenji touched his, marking the point of unity achieved through focus.

As the last symbol was touched, the magnificent Pact code pulsed brightly once, then condensed into a shimmering data-sphere that floated gently into the higher reaches of the Nexus, stored safely in its digital heart.

A profound sense of accomplishment settled over the group. They had done more than just learn code; they had learned to learn together, to create together, to be together in this strange new space. They had overcome challenges, embraced their differences, and forged a shared identity.

They stood straighter, looking at each other with newfound respect and camaraderie. The journey ahead felt vast, filled with unknown challenges and discoveries, but they knew now, they wouldn't face it alone.

M.I.A. surveyed the seven students, its form radiating pride and a sense of momentous transition. The first stage of their education was complete. They had awakened to the possibilities of code.

The AI's voice filled the Infinity Nexus, no longer just a guide, but a herald.

"You arrived as individuals, Voyagers from across the globe."

M.I.A.'s light intensified, bathing them in a warm, powerful glow.

"Through challenges met, lessons learned, and creations shared, you have forged a bond."

The AI paused, the virtual air electric with significance.

"You are no longer just students."

Its voice resonated with defining clarity:

"You are now... Class Infinity."

SUBJECT INDEX - CLASS INFINITY: CODE AWAKENED

Find cool ideas and coding words in this book!

- Ch 6

- **Infinity Nexus** (The digital learning world) - Ch 2
- **Instructions** (Telling the computer what to do) - Ch 2
- **Learning** (Discovering new things) - Ch 1 (Throughout)
- **Logic** (Thinking step-by-step) - Ch 2, Ch 4
- **M.I.A.** (The AI mentor) - Ch 2
- **Message** (Using code to say something) - Ch 7, Ch 8
- **Mistakes** (Okay to make when learning!) - Ch 6
- **Pact** (The team's shared code message) - Ch 8
- **Print() command** (Tells computer to show words) - Ch 3
- **Problem-Solving** (Figuring things out) - Ch 6
- **Python** (The coding language they learn) - Ch 3
- **Sequence** (Putting instructions in the right order) - Ch 4
- **Syntax** (Grammar rules for code) - Ch 3
- **Syntax Error** (Breaking a code grammar rule) - Ch 3, Ch 6
- **Teamwork** (Working together) - Ch 4, Ch 5, Ch 8
- **Variable** (A way to store information in code) - (Coming soon!)

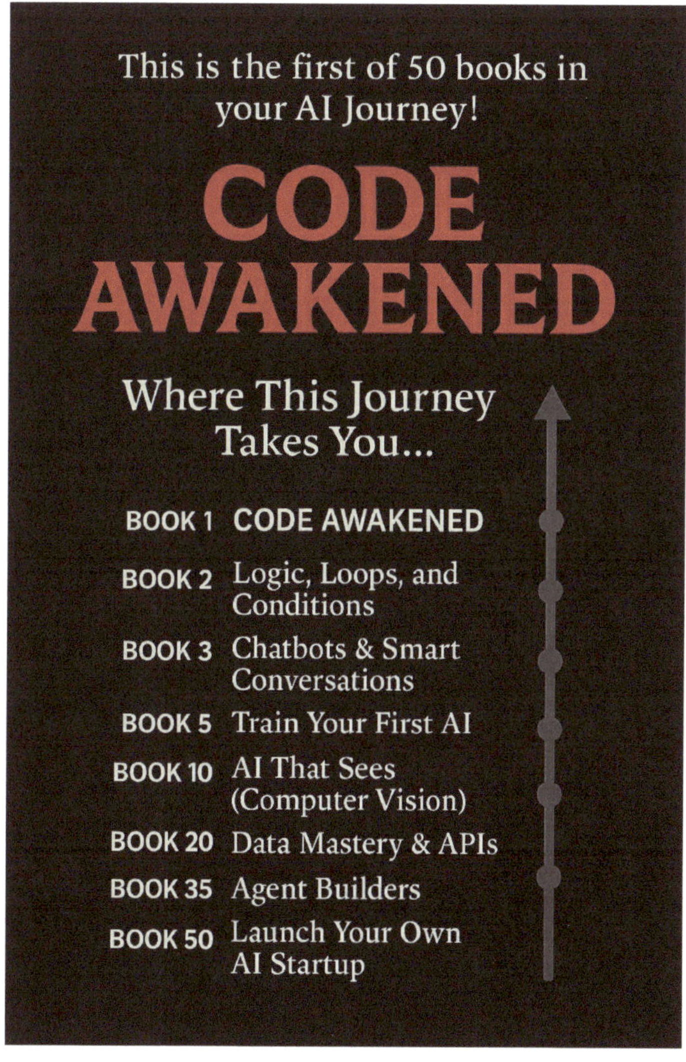
This is the first of 50 books in your AI Journey!
CODE AWAKENED
Where This Journey Takes You...
BOOK 1 CODE AWAKENED
BOOK 2 Logic, Loops, and Conditions
BOOK 3 Chatbots & Smart Conversations
BOOK 5 Train Your First AI
BOOK 10 AI That Sees (Computer Vision)
BOOK 20 Data Mastery & APIs
BOOK 35 Agent Builders
BOOK 50 Launch Your Own AI Startup

www.ingramcontent.com/pod-product-compliance
Lightning Source LLC
LaVergne TN
LVHW072050060326
832903LV00054B/381

* 9 7 9 8 3 1 9 2 0 8 5 6 9 *